Meditations on Quixote

JOSÉ ORTEGA Y GASSET

MEDITATIONS
ON QUIXOTE

TRANSLATED FROM THE SPANISH
BY EVELYN RUGG AND DIEGO MARÍN

INTRODUCTION AND NOTES
BY JULIÁN MARÍAS

UNIVERSITY OF ILLINOIS PRESS
Urbana and Chicago

FIRST ILLINOIS PAPERBACK EDITION, 2000

The "First Meditation: A Short Treatise on the Novel" is reprinted
by permission from *The Hudson Review* 10:1 (Spring 1957), where it
appeared under the title "The Nature of the Novel." © 1957 by
The Hudson Review, Inc.

Library of Congress Cataloging-in-Publication Data
Ortega y Gasset, José, 1883–1955.
[Meditaciones del Quijote. English]
Meditations on Quixote / José Ortega y Gasset ; translated from the
Spanish by Evelyn Rugg and Diego Martín ; introduction and notes
by Julián Marías.
p. cm.
Originally published: New York: W. W. Norton, 1961.
Includes bibliographical references.
ISBN 0-252-06895-5 (alk. paper)
1. Cervantes, Saavedra, Miguel de, 1547–1616. Don Quixote.
2. Aesthetics. 3. Fiction. I. Marías, Julián, 1914– II. Rugg, Evelyn.
III. Marín, Diego. IV. Title.
PQ6352.O67813   2000
863'.3—dc21   99-057812
P 5 4 3 2 1

University of Illinois Press
1325 South Oak Street
Champaign, IL 61820-6903
www.press.uillinois.edu

Contents

6 CONTENTS

Translators' Note

IN justice to Ortega y Gasset's brilliant style, it should be stated that the main aim of this translation has been to convey his thoughts as faithfully as possible in plain English. We have had to sacrifice some of the striking metaphors and figurative phrasing which enrich and enliven the diction of this great master of Spanish prose so that the form would not unduly distract attention from the content.

The Introduction and Notes by Julián Marías, Ortega's foremost disciple and commentator, were published in his extensively annotated edition of the *Meditaciones del Quijote* (Madrid, 1957). His purpose is to show the importance of this early and neglected book which contains in embryonic form much of Ortega's philosophical thought as well as illuminating observations on the art of the novel. It has been possible to include only a small portion of the Commentary. For those interested in exploring further the implications of Ortega's ideas contained in this volume no better guide can be suggested than Marías' complete Commentary in the above edition.

The text of the *Meditaciones del Quijote* used in this translation is that of the *Obras completas* (Madrid, 1946–1947). This edition differs from the first edition (1914) in some footnotes only.

We should like to express our appreciation of the assistance given in our task by the late Professor G. C. Patterson of the Department of Italian and Hispanic

Studies, University of Toronto. We wish to thank the *Hudson Review* for allowing us to use our translation of the "First Meditation," published in it as "The Nature of the Novel" (Spring, 1957).

University of Toronto,   E.R.
                                                           D.M.

Prologue for American Readers

ORTEGA Y GASSET's image abroad has been in many ways different from his image prevailing in Spain. Ortega's first translated book was *The Modern Theme*: he said of himself he was not "modern" but "twentieth-century." And this was a rather difficult book, whose meaning and scope were not easy to grasp at once. Then, and above all, there was *The Revolt of the Masses*, one of the most famous books of this century, a best-seller in a score of languages, whose title was even an entry in some dictionaries; one of the most misunderstood books of our time. Ortega became for the general reader "the author of *The Revolt of the Masses*," an ambiguous surname.

His first book, *Meditations on Quixote*, written in 1914, was never translated into any language. During his whole lifetime, Ortega's hundreds of thousands of foreign readers did not know where he started from. This would be of minor importance if the *Meditations* were just one of his works, perhaps an immature one; but this small book happens to be a masterpiece. It includes—delightfully written—new philosophical theories which anticipate a large part of European thought in the twenties, thirties, and forties; and some others that are not to be found anywhere else.

One could expect to find these ideas in his other, later books. But, even if this proves to be true, the *Meditations* remain of capital importance: because Ortega's thought was deliberately circumstantial, emerging from a definite

9

situation which alone explains and justifies it. The original source of Ortega's philosophy can only be discovered in this meditation on the novel of Cervantes, seen as a key for understanding Spain.

With this book, Ortega began a series of "salvations" which at the same time were "experiments in search of a new Spain." A theory of the novel, the epic, comedy and tragedy unveils the meaning of man as a "hero," who fights with his environment and tries to achieve the humanization of his surroundings in order to make a *world* out of them, while material things press heavily upon him with their meaninglessness and absurdity, trying to suffocate the flame of his projects and aspirations. This permanent and always undecided struggle is human life.

Don Quixote is the symbol of this. His figure, fighting with the windmills on the waste land of Spain, against a glowing sky, is both tragedy and comedy, irony and heroism, unavoidable defeat and unfailing courage. Ortega dives into the depths of *Don Quixote* and comes back to the surface with a rare pearl between his teeth: an interpretation of Spain which includes, as a metaphysical core, one of the most powerful and original philosophies of our time.

Madrid, April, 1960   Julián Marías

Introduction by Julián Marías

ORTEGA'S FIRST BOOK

"THE PRINTING of this book was completed by the Imprenta Clásica Española in Madrid on July 21, 1914." A few days later, while the book was being distributed by the Spanish booksellers and a few curious individuals were cutting the pages of the thin volume—between white paper covers lettered in green—the horizons of Europe were aflame from Flanders to the Masurian Lakes, from Jutland to the Dardanelles: the European War had begun.

This book was the first by its author, José Ortega y Gasset. Its title was preceded by a more general one, *Meditations;* and as many as ten were announced on the back of the title page, forming a complete series. These *Meditations on Quixote* were only the first volume, in fact only half a book, the preliminary meditation and the first one, to be followed by two more; a prologue was placed before all of it, introduced by a friendly vocative: "Reader . . ."

The fact that the *Meditations* were a starting-point is worth emphasizing. It is not immaterial that Ortega should publish a first book; still less so that he should begin to *publish books.* Ortega's intellectual production was already considerable: since 1902 he had written numerous articles, long and short, several of them important. In

1914, however, he addressed the public in a new fashion, beginning with this sentence: "Under the title of *Meditations* this first volume announces several essays on various subjects to be published by a professor of Philosophy *in partibus infidelium*." Ortega presents himself, for the first time, as a professor of Philosophy, which he had been for six years at the Higher Normal School, and then from 1910 in the chair of Metaphysics at the University of Madrid. Some months before, on March 23, 1914, he had given in the Comedia Theater of Madrid the famous lecture *Vieja y nueva política* (Old and New Politics), his first intervention in public life. Clearly this is the moment when Ortega, to use an expression which he repeated frequently, decides to "sign up." He had been born in Madrid on May 9, 1883; he had just passed thirty, the age at which, according to Ortega, the historical activity of a man really begins.

In spite of having been published at such an early date, the *Meditations* have not yet been properly understood and utilized. To explain adequately why this has been so would take us very far and at this moment it would be premature. The book, which has *Quixote* for its theme, says very little about *Quixote;* what it does say of it, however, is of such scope that it has been seized upon and utilized—with or without acknowledgment—by almost all those who have dealt with Cervantes since. The second and third meditations, which were to be devoted more fully to *Quixote* under the somewhat enigmatic titles: "¿Cómo Miguel de Cervantes solía ver el mundo?" (How was Miguel de Cervantes accustomed to view the world?) and "El alcionismo de Cervantes" (The halcyonism of Cervantes), were not published. The first one, "Breve tratado de la novela" (A short treatise on the novel), has usually seemed to be a comparative study of this literary genre with others (epic, tragedy, comedy), an esthetic essay anticipating so many others, especially his "Ideas sobre la novela" (Ideas on the Novel), which were to be published in 1925 with *La deshumanización del arte* (The Dehumanization of Art). As for the prologue and the preliminary meditation, people did not quite know what to do with them. There was undoubtedly philosophy in these pages, but what philosophy? The literary nature of this piece of writing and its connection with the Quixotic theme apparently proved to be misleading.

Towards 1932, when the book had been out for eighteen years—therefore not with undue impatience—Ortega began to call attention to it modestly. In the prologue to the first edition of his works, he repeated: "I am myself plus my circumstance," and he commented: "This expression, which appears in my first book and which sums up my philosophical thought . . ." After some precise explanations he concluded: "Today they have discovered this truth in Germany and some of my compatriots are now realizing it; but it is an incontrovertible fact that it was first thought in Spanish towards 1914." In April of the same year (1932), in his article "Pidiendo un Goethe desde dentro" (In Search of Goethe from Within),* published in the *Revista de Occidente*, Ortega referred in a note to his relations with Heidegger: "I am indebted but little to this author" and gave a detailed account of capital discoveries made in his own *Meditations*. "On occasion," he wrote with restrained melancholy, "I am surprised that not even those nearest to me have the remotest notion of what I have thought and written. Distracted by my images they have glided over my thoughts. . . . To find in this note things like those I am putting down may, perhaps, shame a little those young people who were

* *Partisan Review*, vol. XVI, no. 12, Dec., 1949, 1163–1188. (Translators' note)

ignorant of them in *good faith*. If they were acting in *bad faith* the matter would not be important; the serious thing for them is to discover that they did not know it in good faith, and that, therefore, their own good faith becomes questionable for them. . . . As I have been silent for many years, so I shall remain again for as many more, after the brief interruption of this note, which simply leads every distracted good faith toward the right track."

What were the results of these warnings? Even in his last years Ortega believed he could repeat similar expressions, since the exceptions which would have to be made were so few and obvious that they did not compel him to mitigate the slight exaggeration of general formulas, stylistically justified. I have the impression that some distracted people of good faith felt provoked by Ortega's note to persevere indefinitely in their distraction. There were others who turned back eagerly to the text of the *Meditations* to check on the discoveries which Ortega pointed out: they were there. The majority, however, limited themselves to that homage, and, therefore, saw only what the author had underlined, and, above all, they saw it disconnectedly. Finally, there were those who saw sagaciously that in the *Meditations* there was, outlined at least, a whole philosophy, placed, as an introduction, before the study on Cervantes. When Ortega called attention to the *Meditations*, I, who was born the year of its publication, was beginning to penetrate his work. It is not to be wondered at that I read it attentively, enlightened at the same time by his courses at the University. In 1944, when I met Ortega in Lisbon after eight years, he was surprised that I had understood an essential thesis of the *Meditations*, perhaps the deepest and most difficult in the book. Nevertheless, I now see that I had not completely understood it. Why?

The temptation, even in the best cases, was to *look for the philosophy* in the *Meditations*, thus interpreting, for instance, the prologue and the preliminary meditation as a theory of reality and of knowledge, which ought to be substantified and read independently of its literary context. This, in the last analysis, is insufficient, because the whole book is philosophical, and to look for the philosophy *in it* is to lose its greater and better part; above all, to lose its original and typical *form*, its very peculiar method of *being present* in that book. The thesis to which I have referred, even correctly understood, only acquired its complete significance when placed in relation with other passages—actually in the most "literary" part—which were those that, in a way hitherto unknown, came to consolidate and vivify the "philosophical" theses. These were basically philosophical and therefore true only within the whole context.

Before reading the *Meditations*, it is imperative to step back and ask oneself with some precision how they must be read; or, if one prefers, what reading means in terms of this book, which really means in terms of the new philosophy which starts with this book.

This is less strange than it appears. The author of a philosophical work always plans a definite task, but now and then that aim undergoes an inflection: then we say that a change has been produced in the literary genre of philosophy.* But it is necessary to see this also from the point of view of the reader. The way of reading depends on the literary genre, and when the latter varies, an optical adjustment and at times a difficult apprenticeship is needed. When a philosopher begins this kind of innovation, the immediate result is the improbability that people will know how to read it. It suffices to think of Plato,

* See Julián Marías, "Los géneros literarios en filosofía," in *Ensayos de teoría, Barcelona,* 1954.

Saint Augustine, Descartes, Hegel. The last time that this had occurred, a few years before Ortega, was with Husserl, who required an optical adjustment still difficult today. When the author cannot or does not wish to give the necessary directions so that the reader may carry out that adjustment by himself, he runs the risk of never being read properly and consequently not understood either. At times the deficiency is in the readers, probably not as individuals, but as members of a society which imposes certain usages upon them. In the case of Ortega it is necessary to ask with the greatest possible exactness how those two factors intervene.

If one looks carefully, Ortega gave sufficient directions in the *Meditations;* perhaps the same thing could not be said of other later works, in which the lines guiding the interpretation are not sufficiently explicit, considering the evolution of the doctrine and the degree of precision reached in them. In the *Meditations* he said all there was to be said, and even perhaps more than was necessary, probably because he had in mind the lack of theorizing habits in the Spanish society of his time; but he was not heeded, he was not taken seriously. I think that the cause of this was, first, a lack of sensitivity to the specifically intellectual and philosophical problems. As Ortega had already written in 1907 in his article "Teoría del clasicismo" (Theory of Classicism): "For the one for whom the problems do not exist, the solutions are artificial, forced and paradoxical." The level of the *Meditations* was too exacting: the answers were glided over because the meaning of the questions was not understood, because the curved hooks of the interrogations were missing. Afterwards, on the contrary, when the Spanish mind got accustomed to certain academic and somewhat pedantic kinds of doctrine, people missed the scholarly apparatus and the "technical terminology," and overlooked a theory that was unsuspectedly innovating just because its form—literary structure and style—appeared "inadequate," being considered, as it was, with archaic eyes, without realizing that the form was an essential part of the philosophical innovation.

The first thing that must be borne in mind when reading the *Meditations* is the "argument" of this book: its very existence in a philosophical book is already the beginning of Ortega's most important discovery. The *dramatic* structure of every composition of his—lecture, article, essay, book—forms an unavoidable requisite, a factor essential to its truth and its communicative efficacy. The expression "I am myself plus my circumstance," Ortega will say in 1932, "does not mean only the doctrine which my work expounds and propounds, but also that my work is an active example of that same doctrine. My work is, by essence and presence, circumstantial. By this I mean that it is purposefully so, because without purpose, and even against any contrary purpose, it is obvious that man has never done anything at all in the world that was not circumstantial."

The failure to see this has prevented reading the *Meditations* correctly. When, guided by Ortega's finger, the most sagacious readers have found in its pages certain serious philosophical theses, they have had the impression that they were disconnected. At best, they appeared as glimpses, sudden flashes of insight, still immature or at least not elaborated. Others have considered them as mere "bright ideas," to which only a later exegesis gave philosophical scope. The truth is exactly the opposite: the philosophical doctrine which is expounded in the *Meditations* is perfectly coherent; the connection between its statements, far from being nonexistent, is closely woven, almost excessively so, because it is a real and vital connection, not merely theoretical, that is, an abstraction, a simplification which makes visible the schematic lines of what is, in reality, much more complex, dense, and interlocking. The mere logical argument, the simple "concatenation" of elements, is replaced in this book, as in all Ortega's later work, by something more compact, because the effective connections between real elements are not a "chain," but the systematic and reciprocal vivification of the ingredients in a circumstantial and concrete drama. The function of the elements can only be discovered from the "argument"—characters, settings, feelings, static relationships—of any dramatic structure. *The theory is just another dramatic structure.* Of course, it has always been so; Ortega did not arrange it that way, but he saw and adopted this inevitable condition. From the time of this book onwards, that condition forms an integral part of his theory; or, if it is preferred, from the *Meditations* onwards his theory is intrinsically dramatic.

For this reason any fragmentation of the *Meditations* is a mistake; it must be read as a whole, keeping every thread in mind, without the convenience of "conclusions" on which one can rest, linking them up afterwards as separate, independent units. I mean that the relative inertia of the logical argumentation as used up till now is not allowed, but all the components of the book are to be present in our understanding, acting on it, in a living and operative manner. In other words, the structure of the argumentation of this book belongs to that alert logic, always on the watch, never mechanized and algebraic, which does not tolerate the "lapses" of intellection contained in all abstract thought and excludes all gaps in the evidence: the still-distant logic of concrete thought or, under another name, *vital* reason.

Hence the strange difficulty of a book as easy as this one. Ortega's prose reached one of its peaks in it, the first in point of time. Everything flows in it like a river of transparent water; one goes from proof to proof, from clarity to clarity, impelled by the caressing current of the images, and yet the book itself escapes, one loses a foothold in midstream, its limpid water slipping away between one's fingers. It cannot be reduced to a scheme because the scheme changes it into something else, precisely because it deprives it of its internal, intrinsic dramatic quality. By making a thought-outline of it, we would make its genre change, which would imply a disturbing *de-generation*. A novel, or a drama, cannot be replaced by another structure without losing it. The only thing that can be done is to follow it in the basic sense of *witnessing the action*.

Before starting the reading, the only thing that is permissible is to precede the text, as in dramatic works, by a list of *dramatis personae;* or at most, as in some very intricate detective stories, a brief characterization of the persons whom the reader is going to meet, taking great care not to anticipate abstractly what those who are ignorant of philosophy demand from it: the dénouement without the drama.

The purpose is to meditate on *Quixote,* not through a whim, nor for pleasure only, nor even out of curiosity or the simple desire to know, but in order to know what we have to reckon with. This requires, first of all, to get out of oneself, and enter into what Ortega is going to call from now on the *circumstance:* "the mute things which are all around us." That circumstance is primarily Spain: "The individual cannot get his bearings in the universe except through his race because he is submerged in it like the drop of water in the traveling cloud." By *race* he understands an historical manner of interpreting reality, an original version of the human. To think is going to be, for Ortega, now and forever, to make "experiments on a new Spain," the only possible way for him to find his bearings in life. *Quixote* represents for Ortega the key to Spanish reality, so problematical and contradictory; in other words, the problem of its destiny. What he does when he devotes himself to Cervantes' book is to concentrate on it "the great question: my God, what is Spain?" He does this because *Quixote* is a profound book, full of references and allusions to the universal meaning of life, and also a book in which that particular way of human existence which is the Spanish way—a possibility often lost—has been presented with maximum intensity, and in which, therefore, can be sought what Ortega elsewhere calls "the iridescent gemlike Spain that could have been."

"One of these essential experiences, the greatest perhaps," he says, "is Cervantes. Here is a Spanish plenitude. Here is a word which we can brandish on every occasion as if it were a lance. Alas! If we only knew with certainty the secret of Cervantes' style, of his manner of approaching things, we would have found out everything, because on these spiritual heights there reigns such indestructible solidarity that a poetic style brings with it philosophical, moral, scientific, and political conceptions. If one day someone were to come and reveal to us the profile of Cervantes' style, it would suffice for us to prolong its lines over our other collective problems and we would awake to a new life. Then, if there is courage and genius amongst us, the new Spanish experiment could be made in its purest form."

"Such were the thoughts," says Ortega a little further on, "that came to me during a spring afternoon in the wood that surrounds the Monastery of the Escorial, our great poem in stone. They prompted my decision to write these essays on *Quixote*." But how to do it?

The two words which are repeated most often in the first pages of the *Meditations*, one explaining the other, are *connection* and *love*. They reveal the desire to turn each thing into the center of the universe, to bind things together, to concentrate one's glance on each one in such a way that the light may strike it with "innumerable reflections." The work of art does not surrender, Ortega will say, to the one who goes straight to it but to the one who tries to capture it as Jericho was captured. "In wide circles, our thoughts and our emotions must keep on pressing in on it slowly, sounding in the air, as it were, imaginary trumpets." This is the initial theme of the book: "salvations" as a literary genre, connection, union, love, or more precisely *amor intellectualis*, essays on intellectual love. But this is just what *philosophy* means. Ortega's first definition of the latter was *the general science of love*. It would be worth dwelling at length upon what this definition entails; here, on the threshold of the book, let it suffice to emphasize this: the question is to know what one has to reckon with, which requires a transfer from oneself to one's circumstance, and this is Spain. In its turn, the latter becomes intelligible through certain of its essential experiences, one of which, the fullest perhaps, is Cervantes; and in order to understand Cervantes' book fundamentally, it must be seen in a framework of connections linking it lovingly with all that makes it fully real and intelligible, which only philosophy can do. It is the need to know what one has to reckon with that demands and imposes the use of philosophy. That was the concrete need Ortega felt as a Spaniard in 1914.

When a philosophy is prompted by a concrete demand, it cannot be just any philosophy, that is, any abstract philosophy. I mean that the result of that demand—the philosophical theory—is conditioned, determined, by that demand itself—the situation that makes it necessary. From this point of view, it is evident that the dénouement is always that of a definite drama, without which it makes no sense, nor is it, therefore, such a dénouement. However, if this word is replaced by its synonym *solution*, many people will have no objection to substantifying it and making it independent of the drama which every problem entails, namely, the need to know what we have to reckon with regarding something. Ortega represents the other extreme of this attitude: his philosophy is *circumstantial* in a double sense, and it is important not to overlook either of its two dimensions.

In the first place, it emerges from a concrete situation, from a Spanish circumstance which must be elucidated, illustrated and, more specifically, illustrated in *Quixote*. It is a philosophy whose vital source, and therefore, whose *justification*, is to be found in that precise circumstance, from which it springs, on which it feeds, and from which it is, at least in principle, inseparable. But, in the second place, if we come to the contents and structure of that philosophy we find that it is a doctrine of love, aiming at linking things, at interweaving them with one another and all of them with one's self. The beloved object is the only thing known, that is *comprehended*, not merely "known." Philosophy, the "general science of love," Ortega says, "represents within the intellectual globe the greatest impetus towards an all-embracing connection." But what kind of connection is it? Not of course, that of erudition, which creates a unity of facts, not in themselves but in the head of an individual. It seems, then, that it would be the unity or connection of facts "in themselves." Here is, however, the eternal stumbling-block of all philosophy, which Ortega avoids in a masterly way from the first pages of his first book.

Can a connection or unity of facts "in themselves" be

simply accepted as the only alternative to the unity which they find in the data-filled head of the scholar as a medley of odds and ends? Let us not forget the point of departure: love. The beloved object, says Ortega, is the *indispensable;* that is to say, when we love something, we think that we cannot do without it, that we cannot accept a life in which we would exist and not the beloved object; in short, that we consider it as part of ourselves. We could say, almost with the same words, that I am not only I but, for the time being, I and the beloved object, I and the indispensable. "There is, therefore, in love an extension of the individuality which absorbs other things into it, which unites them to us. This union and interpenetration enable us to perceive clearly the properties of the beloved object. We see it whole and it is revealed to us in all its worth. Then we observe that the beloved object is, in its turn, part of something else that it requires and to which it is bound, and as this is indispensable for the beloved object, it also becomes indispensable to us. In this way love binds one thing to another and everything to us, in a firm essential structure."

One thing to another and everything to us is the formula. In this deepest sense Ortega's philosophy is still circumstantial, it is so in an intrinsic manner; that is to say, *it consists, as a doctrine, in being circumstantial.* Or one could say, if he preferred, that *to philosophize is to circumstantialize,* to turn what confronts us into circumstance or world, an amorous connection in the perspective of an individual existing at a given point, with its foreground, its background, its larger and smaller elements: its hierarchy, in short.

This brings us back to *Quixote,* which represents a maximum level in the hierarchy of Spanish circumstances. For ethnic reasons—in the sense of a historic race— *Quixote* was the obligatory theme of a meditation mo-

tivated by the question: "What is Spain?" **Now, for**
philosophical reasons, a thought defined by its circum-
stantiality in the sense which I have just explained must be
confronted with Cervantes' book and his character. It
may be seen how little is abandoned to chance or caprice
in this book of Ortega's, apparently literary, in reality
subjected to an adamantine intellectual precision, with its
multiple facets carved by a clear-sighted, exact geometry.

But the story does not finish here. Probably what is
most penetrating theoretically in the *Meditations* is, at
the same time, the most radical and profound justification of its theme, which I have not shown as yet. Already
in this first book Ortega discovers the most unique and
irreducible peculiarity of *human life*, different from any
other reality, and therefore from merely biological life.
I am not referring by any means only to the formula: "I
am myself plus my circumstance," which is just the con-
densed expression of Ortega's basic intuition. This intuition is expanded and articulated into a series of visions
which show the characteristic attributes of human life
as such. The only thing lacking is this name of *human
life*, because Ortega had not reached that final simplicity
with which he has been reproached so much and in which
his greatest profundity lies. The manner of being which
human life possesses becomes visible to Ortega in certain
extreme forms which reveal its most authentic nature.
*The structure of life is revealed to him under the species
of heroism or tragedy*. It is both reality and unreality, a
way of being what it still is not, of living with half the
body outside reality, trying to carry out a project, want-
ing to be oneself, to be authentically that which one is to
be, because one has freely chosen to be thus, a "practical"
originality, the "role" which lends its character to each
individual. All of it appears in this book as a theory of the
hero or of the tragic character, not yet as a theory of

human life. But Ortega takes care to warn us that we are all heroes in some measure, that heroism is not ascribed to certain specific contents of life, that it lies dormant everywhere as a possibility, that the will is the tragic theme. In other words, that heroism and tragedy belong essentially to man, as forms of being in which life rids itself of its merely biological condition and exhibits its true nature. Don Quixote is the paradigm of that nature, the example in which it becomes visible, intelligible, because Cervantes interpreted it, illuminated its *logos*, its meaning, revealed it when he re-created it imaginatively. Don Quixote, who is real, who belongs entirely to reality, inserts in this reality his indomitable will, which is a will for adventure. His is a *frontier nature*, and in it is manifested the very condition of man. In Don Quixote human life is shown free from the elements which normally conceal it; this is the *methodical* justification of the *Meditations*, interpreted as a first approximation to a *metaphysical theory of human life*.

All the rest flows, with the *free necessity* of things human, from the internal connection of those themes which I have just pointed out. The circumstantial and vital—biographical—character of reality makes evident that concrete knowledge is *interpretation*, discovery of a *logos* or meaning of things, based on a vital perspective; and this leads on to a new theory of the *concept*—and, therefore, of the whole of logic—which is perhaps the most elaborate part of the *Meditations*, so much so that still today, at the end of forty-two years, it has not been assimilated, much less surpassed. This notion of the concept as bound to perception, of an active vision, brings Ortega to the now famous interpretation of truth as discovery, unveiling, evidence, *aletheia*, and to something which is much more profound, and which made Ortega rid himself from the beginning of any "existentialism," and head toward metaphysics as a theory of human life: the possibility, clearly glimpsed in these pages, of a *vital reason.*

The basic unity of the *Meditations on Quixote* lies simply in the fact that the author, on confronting a problem, on seeing himself forced to face it, had the surprisingly simple determination to hold on to it and to forge with it his own solution. When a man falls into the water, the water is his problem; the swimmer, instead of searching for something outside, supports himself, in order to float and survive, on the very water which threatens to drown him. There exists no other method than swimming along when our problem is none other than that of *reality,* that is to say, when we are dealing with metaphysics.

Meditations on Quixote

To the Reader

To the Reader

UNDER the title of *Meditations* this first volume announces several essays on various subjects of no very great consequence to be published by a professor of Philosophy *in partibus infidelium.* Some of them, like this series of *Meditations on Quixote,* deal with lofty subjects; others with more modest, even humble, subjects; but they all end by discussing Spanish "circumstances" directly or indirectly. These essays are for the author—like the lecture-room, the newspaper, or politics—different means of carrying on one single activity, of expressing the same feeling of affection. I do not claim that this activity should be recognized as the most important in the world; I consider myself justified when I observe that it is the only one of which I am capable. The devotion which moves me to it is the keenest one which I find in my heart. Reviving the fine name which Spinoza used, I would call it *amor intellectualis.* These are therefore essays in intellectual love. They have no informative value whatever; they are not summaries, either—they are rather what a humanist of the seventeenth century would have called "salvations." [1] What is sought in them is the following: given a fact—a man, a book, a picture, a landscape, an error, a sorrow—to carry it by the shortest route to its fullest significance. We want to place the objects of all kinds which life, in its perpetual surge, throws at our feet like the useless remains of a shipwreck, in such a position that the sun as it strikes them may give off innumerable reflections.

Everything has within it an indication of its possible plenitude. An open and noble soul will feel the ambition to perfect it, to help it, so that it may reach this plenitude. This is love—the love for the perfection of the beloved object.[2]

It often happens in the pictures of Rembrandt that a humble white or gray cloth, a coarse household utensil is found wrapped in a luminous and radiant atmosphere, with which other painters surround only the heads of saints. It is as if he said to us in gentle admonition: "Blessed be things! Love them, love them!" Each thing is a fairy whose inner treasures are concealed beneath poor commonplace garments, a virgin who has to be loved to become fruitful.

The "salvation" is not the same as eulogy or dithyramb; it may contain severe censure. The important thing is that the theme be placed in direct relation with the elementary currents of the spirit, with the classic objects of human preoccupation. Once it becomes interwoven with them it is transfigured, transubstantiated, saved. There is a doctrine of love, consequently, that flows beneath the spiritual ground—rough and harsh at times—of these essays, with a muffled, soft sound as if it were afraid of being heard too clearly.

I suspect that, owing to unknown causes, the inner dwelling of the Spaniards was captured long ago by hate, which remains entrenched there, waging war against the world. Now, hatred is a feeling which leads to the extinction of values. When we hate something, we place between it and ourselves a strong spring of steel which prevents even the fleeting fusion of the object with our spirit. The only part of a thing that exists for us is the point touched by the spring of our hatred; all the rest is either unknown to us or is gradually forgotten, making it alien to us. Each moment the object is shrinking, withering away, losing value. In this way the universe has become for the Spaniard something rigid, dry, sordid and deserted. Our souls go through life scowling at it, suspicious and fugitive, like lean, hungry dogs. Among the pages symbolic of a whole Spanish epoch one will always have to include those terrible pages in which Mateo Alemán sketches the allegory of Discontent.

Love, on the contrary, binds us to things, even if only temporarily. If we ask ourselves what new character an object acquires when it is approached with love, what we feel when we love a woman, when we love science, when we love our country, the first thing we shall find is this: what we say we love appears to us as something indispensable. The beloved object is, for the moment, indispensable. That is to say, we cannot live without it, we cannot accept an existence in which we should be bereft of the beloved object, for we consider it part of ourselves. There is, therefore, in love an extension of the individuality which absorbs other things into it, which unites them to us. This union and interpenetration enables us to acquire a deep understanding of the properties of the beloved object. We see it whole and it is revealed to us in all its worth. Then we observe that the beloved object is, in its turn, part of something else that it requires and to which it is bound, and as this is indispensable for the beloved object, it also becomes indispensable to us. In this way love binds one thing to another and everything to us, in a firm essential structure. Love is a divine architect who, according to Plato, came down to the world ὥστε τὸ πᾶν αὐτὸ αὑτῷ ξυνδεδέσθαι—"so that everything in the universe might be linked together."

Separation means extinction. Hatred which separates, isolates, and pulls apart, dismembers the world and destroys individuality. In the Chaldean myth of Izdubar Nimrod, the goddess Ishtar, half-Juno, half-Aphrodite, seeing herself scorned by him, threatens Anu, god of heaven, with the destruction of all creation by merely suspending for an instant the laws of love which joins all beings together, by a simple pause in the symphony of universal eroticism.

We Spaniards offer life a heart shielded by the armor of rancor, and objects, rebounding from it, are cruelly driven away. For centuries we have been involved in an incessant and progressive collapse of values.

We might say of ourselves what a satiric poet of the seventeenth century said of Murtola, the author of the poem *Della creatione del mondo:*

> Il creator di nulla fece il tutto,
> Costui del tutto un nulla, e in conclusione,
> L'un fece il mondo e l'altro l'ha distrutto.*

In these essays I should like to suggest to readers younger than I, the only ones to whom I can, without being immodest, address myself personally, that they should dispel from their minds any customary animosity and that they should strive to make love again rule the universe. The only means of attempting this that I possess is to present sincerely to them the spectacle of a man impelled by the keen desire to understand. Among the several activities of love there is only one with which I can try to infect others: the eagerness to comprehend. All my aspirations would be satisfied if I succeeded in carving some new facets of an ideal sensibility in that tiny portion of the Spanish soul which is within my reach.

---

* *On the Creation of the World:*
The Creator made everything out of nothing,
This one (man) nothing out of everything, and in conclusion,
The one made the world and the other has destroyed it. [Translators' note]

Things do not interest us because they do not find in us favorable surfaces on which to be reflected, and it is necessary for us to multiply the facets of our mind so that an infinite number of themes may penetrate it.

In a Platonic dialogue this urge to understand is called ἐρωτικὴ μανία, "the madness of love." But even if the urge to understand things were not the original form, the genesis and culmination of all love, I believe that it is its indispensable symptom. I mistrust the love of a man for his friend or his flag when I do not see him make an effort to understand his enemy or the flag of his enemy. I have observed, at least, that we Spaniards find it easier to be aroused by a moral dogma than to open our hearts to the demands of veracity. We are definitely more willing to hand over our free will to a rigid moral attitude than to keep our judgment always open, ready at any moment for the desirable reform and correction. One might say that we embrace the moral imperative like a weapon in order to simplify life for ourselves by destroying immense portions of the globe. With keen vision Nietzsche has detected forms and products of resentment in certain moral attitudes. No product of resentment can evoke our sympathy. Rancor emanates from a sense of inferiority. It is the imaginary suppression of the person whom we cannot actually suppress by our own efforts. The one towards whom we feel resentment bears in our imagination the livid semblance of a corpse: in our minds, we have killed him, annihilated him. Later, when we find him actually sound and unconcerned in reality, he seems to us a refractory corpse, stronger than ourselves, whose very existence is an embodiment of mockery, of disdain towards our weakness.

A wiser course than this anticipatory killing of his enemy by the resentful individual consists in falling under the influence of a moral dogma, so that, intoxicated by a certain heroic fiction, we come to believe that the enemy is utterly mistaken and completely in the wrong. The incident of the battle against the Marcomanni in which Marcus Aurelius put the lions from the circus in front of his troops is well known and symbolic. The enemy retreated in terror, but their leader shouted to them: "Don't be afraid! They are Roman dogs!" Calmed, the frightened men turned back to make a victorious attack. Love fights too, it does not stagnate in the troubled peace of compromise; but it fights lions as lions and gives the name "dog" only to dogs.

This struggle with an enemy who is understood is true tolerance, the proper attitude of every robust soul. Why is it so rare in our race? José de Campos, the eighteenth-century thinker, whose interesting book Azorín has discovered, wrote: "The virtues of tolerance are rare in poor peoples"; that is to say, weak peoples.

I hope that, on reading this, no one will draw the conclusion that I am indifferent to the moral ideal.[3] I don't disdain morality for the sake of toying with ideas. The immoralist doctrines which thus far have come to my knowledge lack common sense. And, to tell the truth, I do not devote my efforts to anything but the attainment of a little common sense. It is out of reverence for the moral ideal that we must fight against its greatest enemies, which are perverse moralities. In my opinion—and not only in mine—all utilitarian moralities are perverse, and a moral code is not cleansed of its utilitarian vice by making its prescriptions more rigid. We should be on our guard against rigidity, the traditional livery of hypocrisy. To align the physiognomic features of goodness according to its rigidity is false, inhuman, immoral. Besides, a moral law which is not utilitarian in itself may still be so if the individual who adopts it uses it in a utilitarian way to make his life easier and more comfortable. A long line of great minds has sought through the centuries to enable us to purify our ethical ideal, making it more and more delicate and complex, more crystalline and more intimate. Thanks to them we have been able to avoid confusing goodness with the material observance of legal rules which have been adopted once and for all. On the contrary, a person appears moral to us only when he tries, before any new action, to renew immediate contact with the ethical value itself. When our acts are decided by virtue of intermediary dogmatic prescriptions, the essence of goodness, exquisite and volatile as the most refined perfume, cannot descend upon them. Only from the vivid and ever new intuition of perfection can this perfume fall directly on our acts. Therefore any moral code which does not include among its injunctions the primary duty of being always ready for the reform, the correction, and the expansion of the ethical ideal will be immoral. Any principle of ethics that enjoins the perpetual seclusion of our free will within a closed system of valuation is *ipso facto* perverse. As in political constitutions of the "open" type, there must be in ethics a principle which encourages the enlargement and enrichment of moral experience. The good is, like nature, an immense landscape in which man advances through centuries of exploration. With acute consciousness of this, Flaubert once wrote: "The ideal is fertile—that is, morally fertile —only when it is all-embracing. It is a work of love and not of exclusion."

Understanding, then, is not opposed in my mind to morality. The opposition lies between a perverse morality and an integral morality, for which understanding is a clear and primary duty. Through this duty our radius of sympathy increases indefinitely, and, as a result, the probability of our being righteous. There is a true religious attitude at the center of the urge to understand, and, as far as I am concerned, I must confess that, when I get up in the morning, I recite a very brief prayer, thousands of years old, a verse from the *Rig-Veda*, which contains these few winged words: "Lord, awaken us in a happy mood and give us knowledge!" Thus prepared, I go through the bright or gloomy hours that come with the day.

Is this call to understand perchance too demanding? Is not understanding a thing the least we can do in its service? And who can be sure, if he is honest with himself, of doing the greater thing without having had knowledge of the lesser?

In this sense I consider philosophy to be the general science of love; it represents the greatest impulse toward an integrated whole within the intellectual sphere, with the result that a shade of difference between understanding and mere knowing becomes apparent in it. We know so many things that we do not understand! All knowledge of facts is really incomprehensive and can be justified only when used in the service of a theory.

Ideally speaking, philosophy is the opposite of information or erudition. Far be it from me to scorn the latter; factual knowledge has doubtless been a form of science. It had its hour. Back in the time of Justus Lipsius, of Huet or of Casaubon, philological knowledge had not found sure methods to discover unity of meaning in the torrential masses of historical facts. Investigation could not be directly the investigation of the unity hidden in the phenomena. There was no other method but to summon at random the greatest possible accumulation of data in the memory of an individual. By thus endowing them with an external unity—a hodgepodge sort of unity— one could expect that some of them might join others in spontaneous associations, from which some light might emerge. This unity of facts, not found in themselves, but in the mind of an individual, is erudition. To go back to it in our age would be tantamount to a retrogression of philosophy, as if chemistry went back to alchemy or medicine to magic. Gradually the mere scholars are becoming rarer and soon we shall witness the disappearance of the last mandarins.

Erudition, then, occupies the outskirts of science because it is limited to accumulating facts, while philosophy represents its central aspiration, because it is pure synthesis. In the accumulating process the data are merely collected, and, forming a heap, each one asserts its independence, its separateness. In the synthesis of facts, on the contrary, the latter disappear like a well-assimilated food and only their essential vigor remains.

The ultimate ambition of philosophy would be to arrive at a single proposition which would express the whole truth.[4] Thus the twelve hundred pages of Hegel's *Logik* are just the preparation which enables us to pronounce, in all the fullness of its meaning, this sentence: "The idea is the absolute." This sentence, so poor in appearance, has in reality a literally infinite meaning; and when one considers it as one should, the whole treasury of its significance bursts open suddenly and it illuminates for us at once the enormous perspective of the world. This supreme illumination I have called understanding. Particular formulas may prove to be erroneous, and even all those that have been tried may be wrong; but from their doctrinal ruins philosophy is reborn intact as an aspiration, as an urge.

Sexual pleasure seems to be a sudden discharge of nervous energy. Esthetic enjoyment is a sudden discharge of allusive emotions. By analogy, philosophy is like a sudden discharge of intellectual insight.

These *Meditations*, free from erudition—even in the best sense of the word—are propelled by philosophical desires. Nevertheless I would be grateful if the reader did not expect too much from them. They are not philosophy, which is a science. They are simply essays. The essay is science, minus the explicit proof. For the writer it is a point of intellectual honor not to write anything susceptible of proof without possessing the latter beforehand. But it is permissible for him to eliminate from his work all apodictic appearance, leaving the verifications merely indicated in ellipse, so that he who needs them may find them and so that they do not hinder, on the other hand, the communication of the inner warmth with which the thoughts were conceived. Even books of an exclusively scientific intention are beginning to be written in a less didactic style with fewer labor-saving aids, with footnotes omitted as far as possible and the rigid mechanical apparatus of proof dissolved in a more organic, flowing, and personal discourse.

With greater reason this should be done in essays of this kind, in which, although for the author the doctrines are scientific convictions, he does not expect the reader to accept them as truths. I only offer *modi res considerandi*, possible new ways of looking at things. I invite the reader to test them for himself, to see if, in fact, they provide fertile visions. He, then, by virtue of his intimate and sincere experience, will test their truth or error.

It is my intention that these ideas serve a function much less serious than a scientific one: they will not stubbornly insist on being adopted by others, but merely wish to awaken in kindred minds kindred thoughts, even though they be antagonistic. They are only a pretext and an appeal for a wide ideological collaboration on national themes, and nothing else.

Along with lofty themes, these *Meditations* deal very frequently with the most insignificant things. Attention is paid to details of the Spanish landscape, of the peasants' way of talking, of the folk dances and songs, of the colors and style in dress and implements, of the peculiarities of the language, and in general of the minute manifestations which reveal the innermost character of a race.

Taking great care not to confuse the great with the small, maintaining always the need for a hierarchy, without which the cosmos returns to chaos, I consider it urgent that we also direct our reflective attention, our meditation, to what is near us.

Man reaches his full capacity when he acquires complete consciousness of his circumstances. Through them he communicates with the universe.

Circumstance! *Circum stantia!*[5] That is, the mute things which are all around us. Very close to us they raise their silent faces with an expression of humility and eagerness as if they needed our acceptance of their offering and at the same time were ashamed of the apparent simplicity of their gift. We walk blindly among them, our gaze fixed on remote enterprises, embarked upon the conquest of distant schematic cities. Few books have moved me as much as those stories in which the hero goes forward, impetuous and straight as an arrow, towards a glorious goal, without noticing the anonymous maiden who, secretly in love with him, walks beside him with a humble and suppliant look, carrying within her white body a heart which burns for him, like a red-hot coal on which incense is burned in his honor. We should like to signal to the hero for him to turn his eyes for a moment towards that passion-inflamed flower which is at his feet. All of us are heroes in varying degrees and we all arouse humble loves around us. "I have been a fighter/ And this means I have been a man," exclaims Goethe. We are heroes, we are forever struggling for something far away, and trample upon fragrant violets as we go.

In my "Essay on Limitation," * I stop to meditate on this theme with leisurely delight. I believe very seriously that one of the most profound changes in the present as compared with the nineteenth century is going to consist in the changing of our sensitivity to environment. A sort of restlessness and impatience seemed to prevail in the past century—in its second half especially—which compelled people to disregard everything immediate and momentary in life. As distance lends a more synthesizing outline to the past century, its essentially political character becomes clearer to us. Western man underwent his apprenticeship in politics, a kind of life hitherto confined to ministers and palace councils. Political preoccupation, that is, consciousness of and activity in the social field, spreads among the masses, thanks to democracy. With a fierce exclusivism the problems of social life took over the first plane of attention, while the other element, individual life, was put aside as a matter of little consequence. It is especially significant that the only powerful affirmation of the individual in the nineteenth century—individualism—should be a political doctrine, that is to say, a social one, and that its whole tenet consisted in asking that the individual should not be annihilated. How can we doubt that some day soon this will appear incredible?

We have devoted all our serious efforts to the administration of society, to the strengthening of the State, to social culture, to social struggles, to the knowledge of science as a technique for enriching collective life. It

* An essay which has never been published. [Translators' note]

would have seemed frivolous to devote a part of our best energies—and not only what was left over—to organize friendship around us, to build up a perfect love, to see in the enjoyment of things a dimension of life which deserves to be cultivated with the best methods; and the same may be said of a multitude of private needs which shamefacedly hide themselves in the corners of our mind because they are not granted their rights, that is, their cultural significance.

In my opinion every need, if it is fully developed, becomes a new cultural area. Man should not always find himself confined to the higher values discovered up to the present: science and justice, art and religion. In due time Pleasure will find its Newton and Ambition its Kant.

Culture presents us with objects already purified which once possessed a spontaneous and immediate life, and which now, thanks to our reflective process, seem free from space and time, from corruption and caprice. They form, as it were, a zone of ideal and abstract life, floating above this personal existence of ours, always so uncertain and problematical. Individual life, the immediate, the circumstance, are different names for the same thing: those parts of life from which their inner spirit, their *logos*, has not yet been extracted. Since spirit and *logos* are nothing but "meaning," connectedness, and unity, all that is individual, immediate, and circumstantial appears to be accidental and meaningless.

We ought to consider that social life as well as the other forms of culture are given to us in the form of individual life, of the immediate. What we today receive already decorated with sublime aureoles once had to contract and shrink in order to pass through a man's heart. All that is recognized today as truth, as perfect beauty, as highly valuable, was once born in the inner spirit of an individual, mixed with his whims and humors. We should not let our acquired culture become hieratic, as it will if we are more concerned with repeating than increasing it.

The specifically cultural act is the creative, that in which we extract the *logos* from something which was still meaningless (*i-logico*). Acquired culture has value only as the instrument and weapon of new conquests. Therefore, in comparison with the immediate, with our spontaneous life, all that we have learned seems to be abstract, generic, schematic. It not only seems so, it is. The hammer is the abstraction of each one of its hammerings.

All that is general, all that has been learned, achieved in culture is only the tactical turn which we have to take in order to cope with the immediate. Those who live near a cataract do not notice its roar; it is necessary for us to put some distance between our immediate surroundings and ourselves so that they may acquire meaning in our eyes.

The Egyptians believed that the valley of the Nile was the whole world. Such a statement about a circumstance is monstrous and, contrary to what it might appear, impoverishes its significance. Certain minds show their basic weakness when they cannot become interested in a thing unless they delude themselves into thinking that it is the whole or the best in the world. This sticky and womanish idealism must be eradicated from our consciousness. Only parts do exist in fact; the whole is an abstraction of the parts and it depends on them. In the same way, there cannot be anything better except where there are other good things, and it is only by our being interested in the latter that the better or best acquires its rank. What is a captain without soldiers?

When shall we open our minds to the conviction that

the ultimate reality of the world is neither matter nor spirit, is no definite thing, but a perspective? [6] God is perspective and hierarchy; Satan's sin was an error of perspective. Now, a perspective is perfected by the multiplication of its viewpoints and the precision with which we react to each one of its planes. The intuition of higher values fertilizes our contact with the lesser ones, and love for what is near and small makes the sublime real and effective within our hearts. For the person for whom small things do not exist, the great is not great.

We must try to find for our circumstance, such as it is, and precisely in its very limitation and peculiarity, its appropriate place in the immense perspective of the world. We must not stop in perpetual ecstasy before hieratic values, but conquer the right place among them for our individual life. In short, the reabsorption of circumstance is the concrete destiny of man.[7]

My natural exit toward the universe is through the mountain passes of the Guadarrama or the plain of Ontígola. This sector of circumstantial reality forms the other half of my person; only through it can I integrate myself and be fully myself. The most recent biological science studies the living organism as a unit composed of the body and its particular environment so that the life process consists not only of the adaptation of the body to its environment but also of the adaptation of the environment to its body. The hand tries to adjust itself to the material object in order to grasp it firmly; but, at the same time, each material object conceals a previous affinity with a particular hand.

I am myself plus my circumstance, and if I do not save it, I cannot save myself.[8] *Benefac loco illi quo natus es,* as we read in the Bible. And in the Platonic school the task of all culture is given as "to save the appearances," the phenomena; that is to say, to look for the meaning of what surrounds us.

Having exercised our eyes in gazing at the world map, let us now concentrate on the Guadarrama. Perhaps we shall find nothing profound, but we may be sure that the defect and the sterility derive from our glance. There is also a *logos* of the Manzanares River: this very humble stream, this liquid irony which laps the foundations of our capital, undoubtedly bears a drop of spirituality among its few drops of water. For there is nothing on earth through which some divine nerve does not pass: the difficulty lies in reaching this nerve and making it react. To the friends who are hesitating to enter his kitchen, Heraclitus cries: "Come in, come in! The gods are here too." Goethe writes to Jacobi on one of his botanical-geological excursions: "Here I am going up and down hills and searching for the divine *in herbis et lapidibus.*" It is told of Rousseau that he used to grow herbs in his canary's cage, and Fabre, who tells about it, writes a book about the tiny creatures which lived on the legs of his desk.

Nothing prevents heroism—which is the activity of the spirit—as much as considering it bound to certain specific contents of life. The possibility of heroism must subsist beneath the surface everywhere, and every man should be able to hope that a spring may come forth when he strikes vigorously the earth he treads. For Moses the Hero, every rock contains a spring. For Giordano Bruno, *est animal sanctum, sacrum et venerabile, mundus.*

Pío Baroja and Azorín are two of our circumstances, and I devote an essay to each of them.* Azorín offers a

* They have appeared in Volumes I and II of *El Espectador,* under the titles 'Ideas sobre Pío Baroja" (*O.C.*, II, 68–100) and "Azorín: primores de lo vulgar" (*O.C.*, II, 154–185). [Translators' note]

chance to meditate from a different angle from the one I have just taken, on the minutiae and on the value of the past. With respect to the minutiae, it is high time for us to overcome the latent modern hypocrisy of pretending to be interested only in certain sacred conventions—science, art, or society—and of reserving, as we were bound to do, the innermost recesses of our being for the trivial and even the physiological. The fact is that when we have reached the depths of pessimism and do not seem to find anything positive enough in the universe to save us, our eyes turn towards the small things of daily living—as dying men remember on the point of death the most trifling things that happened to them. We see, then, that it is not the *great things,* the great pleasures, nor the great ambitions which keep us alive upon the face of the earth, but the moment of comfort near a hearth in winter, the pleasant sensation of a drink of liqueur, the attractive gait of a pretty girl we neither love nor know, the amusing remark and pleasing voice of a witty friend. An incident that strikes me as very human was that of the desperate man who was going to hang himself from a tree, and as he was putting the rope around his neck happened to smell the fragrance of a rose which was at the foot of the tree and refrained from hanging himself.

Here lies one secret of the source of his vitality which, for virtuous living, contemporary man must meditate on and comprehend; today he constrains himself to hide it, to look away from it, as from so many other obscure forces —the sexual urge, for instance—which after much concealment and hypocrisy, end by triumphing in the conduct of his life. The subhuman persists in man: what does that persistence mean to man? What is the *logos,* the clear position which we must take when confronted with that emotion expressed by Shakespeare in one of his comedies, with words so intimate, heartfelt, and sincere that they seem to drip from one of his sonnets? A character in *Measure for Measure* says:

> . . . Yea, my gravity,
> Wherein (let no man hear me) I take pride,
> Could I, with boot, change for an idle plume,
> Which the air beats for vain.

Isn't this an improper desire? And yet . . . !

With respect to the past, the esthetic theme of Azorín, we should see in it one of our terrible national diseases. Kant's *Anthropologie* contains an observation on Spain so profound and so true that it makes one shudder. Kant says that the Turks when they travel usually describe the character of a country according to its typical vice, and that, following this practice, he listed them as follows: 1. Land of fashions (France). 2. Land of bad temper (England). 3. Land of ancestors (Spain). 4. Land of ostentation (Italy). 5. Land of titles (Germany). 6. Land of lords (Poland).

Spain—land of ancestors! Therefore, not ours, not the free property of present-day Spaniards. Those who have gone before continue to rule us and form an oligarchy of the dead, which oppresses us. "Remember," says the servant in the *Choephori*, "the dead kill the living."

This influence of the past on our race is a most delicate question. Through it we shall discover the psychological mechanism of Spanish reactionary propensities. I am not referring to such tendencies in politics, which are only one manifestation, the least profound and significant of the general reactionary constitution of our spirit. We shall see in this essay how true reactionism is not characterized in the last instance by its dislike for modernity, but by its manner of dealing with the past.

Let me use a paradoxical formula for the sake of conciseness: the death of what is dead is life. There is only one way to dominate the past, the realm of things that have perished: to open our veins and inject some of our blood into the empty veins of the dead. This is what the reactionary cannot do: treat the past as a form of life. He pulls it out of the sphere of vitality, and, thoroughly dead as it is, he places it on its throne so that it may rule over our souls. It is not by chance that the Celtiberians attracted attention in ancient times as the only people that worshiped death.

This inability to keep the past alive is the truly reactionary feature. Antipathy towards what is new seems, on the contrary, common to other psychological temperaments. Could one say Rossini was a reactionary because he never wanted to travel by train and went about Europe in his gaily jingling carriage? This attitude becomes serious only when the recesses of our souls are infected and, like birds flying over the miasma of a swamp, the past falls dead within our memories.

In dealing with Pío Baroja we shall have to meditate on happiness and on "action"; in fact we shall have to talk a little about everything, because this man is a crossroads rather than a man. Incidentally, the reader may perhaps think that in this essay on Baroja as well as in those devoted to Goethe and Lope de Vega, to Larra and even in some of these *Meditations on Quixote*, relatively little is said about the concrete theme in question.* They are, in fact, critical studies, but I do not believe that the important mission of criticism is to appraise literary works, dividing them into good or bad. I am becoming less interested every day in passing judgment;

* Besides *Goethe desde dentro* (Goethe from within), 1932, Ortega gave lectures on Goethe in the United States and Germany (1949); his essays on Lope de Vega and Larra were never written, according to Julián Marías. [Translators' note]

I feel more inclined to love things than to judge them.

I see in criticism a fervent effort to bring out the full power of the chosen work. It is just the opposite, then, to what Sainte-Beuve does when he takes us from the work to the author and then sprays him with a shower of anecdotes. Criticism is not biography, nor is it justified as an independent labor unless its purpose is to complete the work. This means first of all that the critic is expected to provide in his work all the sentimental and ideological aids which will enable the ordinary reader to receive the most intense and clearest possible impression of the book. Criticism should have an affirmative aim and rather than being directed toward correcting the author it should try to endow the reader with a more perfect visual organ so that the work is completed by reading it.

Thus, when I speak of a critical study of Pío Baroja, I mean the combination of points of view from which his books acquire a higher significance. It should not be surprising, then, if little is said about the author and even about the details of his production. The purpose is, precisely, to bring together all that is not found in him, but which completes him, giving him the most favorable atmosphere.

In these *Meditations on Quixote* I attempt to make a study of Quixotism. But there is an ambiguity in this word. My Quixotism has nothing to do with the merchandise displayed under such a name in the market. Don Quixote may mean two very different things: *Don Quixote* as a book and Don Quixote as a character from that book. What is generally understood in a good or a bad sense as "Quixotism" is the Quixotism of the character. These essays, however, investigate the Quixotism of the book.

The figure of Don Quixote, set in the middle of the work like an antenna which picks up all the allusions, has attracted exclusive attention, to the detriment of the rest of the book and, consequently, to that of the character himself. It is true that with a little love and also a little modesty—certainly not without both—one might compose a subtle parody on the *Names of Christ*, that fine book of Romanesque symbolism which Fray Luis de León composed with theological zest in the orchard of La Flecha. One could write the *Names of Don Quixote*, because in a certain way, Don Quixote is the sad parody of a more divine and serene Christ: he is a Gothic Christ, torn by modern anguish; a ridiculous Christ of our own neighborhood, created by a sorrowful imagination which lost its innocence and its will and is striving to replace them. Whenever a few Spaniards who have been sensitized by the idealized poverty of their past, the sordidness of their present, and the bitter hostility of their future gather together, Don Quixote descends among them and the burning ardor of his crazed countenance harmonizes those discordant hearts, strings them together like a spiritual thread, nationalizes them, putting a common racial sorrow above their personal bitterness. "For where two or three are gathered together in my name," said Jesus, "there am I in the midst of them."

Nevertheless, the errors to which the isolated consideration of Don Quixote has led are really grotesque. Some, with charming foresight, advise us not to be Don Quixotes; others, following the latest fashion, invite us to an absurd existence, full of extravagant gestures. For all of them, apparently, Cervantes did not exist. Yet Cervantes came upon this earth to carry our minds beyond that dualism.

We cannot understand the individual except through his kind. Real things are made of matter or energy, but artistic things—like the character of Don Quixote—are made of a substance called style. Each esthetic object is the individualization of a style-protoplasm. Thus, the individual Don Quixote is an individual of the Cervantes species.

It is wise, then, for us to make an effort and divert our attention from Don Quixote, examining the rest of the book so as to gain from its vast surface a broader and clearer notion of the Cervantine style, of which the Manchegan knight is only one particular embodiment. For me the real Quixotism is that of Cervantes, not that of Don Quixote; and not that of Cervantes in the prison of Algiers or in his life, but *in* his book. In order to avoid this biographical and learned deflection, I prefer the title Quixotism to Cervantism.

The task is so lofty that the author undertakes it as sure of his defeat as if he were going to fight with the gods. Secrets are wrested from Nature in a violent way. After getting his bearings in the cosmic forest, the scientist goes straight to the problem like a hunter. For Plato, as for St. Thomas, the man of science is a man who goes hunting, θηρευτής, *venator*. If he possesses the weapon and the will, his game is won; so the new truth will inevitably fall at his feet, like a bird wounded in flight. But the secret of an artistic masterpiece does not yield to intellectual attack in this way. It might be said that it is reluctant to be taken by force, and only yields to whom it chooses. It requires, like scientific truth, that we devote laborious attention to it, but without our going straight at it, like hunters. It does not surrender to weapons: it surrenders, if at all, to the meditative cult. A work as great as *Quixote* has to be taken as Jericho was taken. In wide circles, our thoughts and our emotions must keep on pressing in on it slowly, sounding in the air, as it were, imaginary trumpets.

Cervantes—a patient gentleman who wrote a book—has been sitting in the Elysian fields for three centuries and gazing sadly around, awaiting the birth of a grandson capable of understanding him. These meditations, which will be followed by others, do not, of course, pretend to invade the ultimate secrets of *Quixote*. They are wide circles of attention which our thought describes without haste and at some distance, fatally attracted by the immortal work.

And now a final word. I expect the reader will discover, even in the hidden corners of these essays, the throbs of a patriotic preoccupation. The author who is writing them and those to whom they are addressed have their spiritual origin in the denial of a decrepit Spain. But denial by itself is impious. When the pious and honest man denies something, he assumes the obligation to set up a new proposition, or at least to try to do so. We do too. Having denied one Spain, honor bids us find another and will not let us rest until we do so. Therefore, if we were observed in our most intimate and personal meditations, we should be found trying out experiments on a new Spain with the humblest fibers of our soul.

Preliminary Meditation

Preliminary Meditation

"Ist etwa der *Don Quixote* nur eine Posse?" *

THE MONASTERY of the Escorial rises on a hill. The south side of this hill slopes down under the covering of a grove of both oak and ash trees. The site is called "La Herrería," the Smithy. The character of the superb gray mass of the building changes with the season, for the thick blanket of vegetation spread out at its feet is copper-hued in winter, golden in autumn and dark green in summer. Spring passes through here swiftly, instantaneously and exuberantly—like an erotic image through the steely soul of a monk. The trees are rapidly covered with luxuriant masses of leaves of a bright fresh green; the ground disappears under an emerald grass which, in its turn, is bedecked one day with the yellow of daisies, another day with the purple of lavender. There are places which enjoy a wonderful silence—which is never absolute silence. When all around is completely quiet, the noiseless void which remains must be occupied by something, and then we hear the pounding of our own hearts, the throbbing of the blood in our temples, the flow of air which floods into our lungs and then rushes out. All this is disturbing because it has too concrete a meaning. Each heartbeat sounds as if it were to be our last. The following beat which saves us always seems to come accidentally and

* Is *Don Quixote* only a farce, perchance? (Hermann Cohen: *Ethik des reinen Willens*, p. 487). [Translators' note]

57

does not guarantee the next one. That is why it is preferable to have a silence in which purely decorative, unidentifiable sounds are heard. This place is like that; it is crisscrossed by clear murmuring streams, and small birds sing amid its verdure—greenfinches, linnets, orioles, and an occasional sublime nightingale.

On one such afternoon of the fleeting spring, the following thoughts came to meet me in "La Herrería."

1

The Forest[9]

How many trees make up a forest? How many houses a city? As the peasant from Poitiers sang,

> La hauteur des maisons
> empêche de voir la ville,

or, as the Germanic proverb goes, one cannot see the forest for the trees. Forest and city are two things essentially deep, and depth is fatally condemned to become a surface if it wants to be visible.

I have now around me as many as two dozen grave oaks and graceful ashes. Is this a forest? Certainly not. What I see here is some trees of the forest. The real forest is composed of the trees which I do not see. The forest is invisible nature—hence the halo of mystery its name preserves in all languages. I can now get up and take one of these blurred trails ahead of me, crisscrossed by the blackbirds. The trees which I saw before will be replaced by similar ones. The forest will be breaking up into a series of successively visible portions, but I shall never find it where I am. The forest flees from one's eyes.

When we arrive at a small clearing in the verdure, it seems as if a man had been sitting there on a stone, with his elbows on his knees, his hands on his temples, and that just as we were arriving he had got up and left. We suspect that this man, taking a short roundabout course, has gone to take up the same position not far from us. If we yield to the desire to surprise him—to that power of attraction which the center of forests exerts on those who enter them, the scene will be repeated indefinitely.

The forest is always a little beyond where we are. It has just gone away from where we are and all that remains is its still fresh trace. The ancients, who projected their emotions into corporeal and living forms, peopled the forests with fugitive nymphs. Nothing could be more exact and expressive. As you walk along, glance quickly at a clearing in the bush and you will notice a quivering of the air as if it were hastening to fill the void left by the sudden departure of a slender, naked form.

From any spot within its borders the forest is just a possibility: a path along which we could proceed, a spring from which a gentle murmur is brought to us in the arms of silence and which we might discover a few steps away, snatches of songs sung in the distance by birds perched on branches under which we could pass. The forest is the aggregate of possible acts of ours which, when carried out, would lose their real value. The part of the forest immediately before us is a screen, as it were, behind which the rest of it lies hidden and aloof.

2

Depth and Surface

WHEN one repeats the sentence "one cannot see the forest for the trees," its exact meaning is perhaps not understood. It may be that the intended joke turns its point against the speaker. The trees do not allow the forest to be seen, and it is due to this fact that the forest exists. The function of the visible trees is to make the rest of them latent, and only when we fully realize that the visible landscape is concealing other invisible landscapes do we feel that we are in a forest.

This invisibility, this being hidden, is not a merely negative quality, but a positive one which transforms the thing it hides, making a new thing of it. In this sense it is absurd to try to see the forest, as the aforementioned saying declares. The forest is the latent as such.

There is a good lesson here for those who do not see the multiplicity of individual destinies, all equally respectable and necessary, which the world contains. There are things which, when revealed openly, succumb or lose their value and, on the other hand, reach their fullness when they are hidden or overlooked. There are men who might reach complete self-fulfillment in a secondary position, but whose eagerness to occupy the forefront destroys all their worth. A contemporary novel presents a certain boy, not very intelligent but endowed with an exquisite moral sensibility, who consoles himself for being the last in his class by thinking: "After all, someone has to be the last!" This is a good remark, good enough to guide us. There may be as much nobility in being

61

last as in being first, because the two positions are equally necessary in the world, the one to complement the other.

Some men refuse to recognize the depth of something because they demand that the profound should manifest itself in the same way as the superficial. Not accepting the fact that there may be several kinds of clarity, they pay exclusive attention to the clarity peculiar to surfaces. They do not realize that to be hidden beneath the surface, merely appearing through it, throbbing underneath it, is essential to depth.

To ignore the fact that each thing has a character of its own and not what we wish to demand of it, is in my opinion the real capital sin, which I call a sin of the heart because it derives its nature from lack of love. There is nothing so illicit as to dwarf the world by means of our manias and blindness, to minimize reality, to suppress mentally fragments of what exists. This happens when one demands that what is deep should appear in the same way as what is superficial. No, there are things which present only that part of themselves which is strictly necessary to enable us to realize that they lie concealed behind it. In order to find evidence of this, it is not necessary to mention anything very abstract. All deep things are similarly constituted. The material objects which we see and touch, for example, have a third dimension which constitutes their depth, their inwardness. However, we do not see or touch this third dimension. We find on their surfaces, it is true, suggestions of something which lies within; but what is within can never come forth and become visible in the same way as what is without. It will be useless for us to begin to break up the third dimension into superficial layers: no matter how thin the slices may be, the layers will always have some thickness, that is to say, some depth, some invisible, intangible inwardness. And if we succeed in obtaining layers so thin that our eyes can see through them, then we do not see either the depth or the surface, but a perfect transparency, or, what is the same thing, nothing. For just as depth needs a surface beneath which to be concealed, the surface or outer cover, in order to be so, needs something over which to spread, covering it.

This truth is all too obvious, but it is not completely useless, because there are still some people who demand that we make them see everything as clearly as they see an orange before their eyes. But actually, if seeing is understood as a merely sensorial function, neither they nor anyone else has ever seen an orange in their terms. The latter is a spherical body, therefore with an obverse and a reverse. Can anybody claim to have the obverse and the reverse of an orange in front of him at the same time? With our eyes we see one part of the orange, but the entire fruit is never presented to us in a perceptible form; the larger portion of the orange is concealed from our eyes.

There is no need, therefore, to have recourse to subtle and metaphysical matters to indicate that things have different ways of presenting themselves, but each one in its own way is equally clear. What is seen is not the only thing that is clear. The third dimension of a body is offered to us with as much clarity as the other two dimensions, and yet things or certain of their qualities would not exist for us if there were no other methods of seeing than the passive method of vision in the strict sense.

3

Streams and Orioles

Our thought is now a dialectical faun pursuing the essence of the forest as if it were chasing a fleeing nymph. In contact with the naked body of an idea it experiences a sort of amorous delight. Having recognized as the fleeting nature of the forest, always absent, always concealed —an ensemble of possibilities—our idea of the forest is not yet complete. If the deep and latent is to exist for us it must manifest itself to us, and do so in such a form that it does not lose its depth or its latency. As I said before, depth suffers the inevitable fate of showing itself through superficial features. Let us see how it does so.

This water which is flowing at my feet complains gently as it strikes the pebbles and forms a curved arm of crystal around the root of this oak tree. Just now an oriole has entered the oak tree as a king's daughter enters her palace. From the oriole's throat comes a deep warble, so musical that it seems a note snatched from the nightingale's song, a short sudden sound which fills the visible area of the forest completely for an instant, just as a pang of sorrow suddenly fills the area of our consciousness.

Now I have two sounds before me, but they are not alone. They are merely lines or dots of sound which stand out above a multitude of other murmurs and sounds interwoven with them because of their genuine fullness and their peculiar brilliance. If from the song of an oriole perched over my head and the sound of the water which flows at my feet I let my attention wander to other sounds, I hear again an oriole's song and a murmuring of water as it struggles along in its stony bed. But what happens to these new sounds? I recognize one of them without hesitation as the oriole's song, but it lacks brightness, purpose. Its piercing sound does not strike the air with the same energy, it does not fill the atmosphere in the same way as the first one but, rather, it slips by surreptitiously, timidly. I recognize also this second sound of water, but, alas, what a pitiful sound it is! Is it an ailing spring? It is a sound like the previous one, but more halting, more like a sob, less rich in inner resonance, somewhat muffled, blurred, and sometimes not strong enough to reach my ear; it is a poor, weak murmur that stumbles along.

Such is the effect of these new sounds considered as only impressions. But I, on hearing them, did not stop to describe their mere presence, as I have done here. Without having to think, as soon as I hear them I wrap them up in an act of ideal interpretation and throw them away from me. I hear them as if they were distant. If I limit myself to receiving them passively in my hearing, these two pairs of sounds are equally present and near. But the difference in the sound quality of the two pairs stimulates me to put them at a distance, attributing to each a different spacial quality. It is I, then, by an act of mine, who keeps them virtually separated: if this act were lacking, the distance would disappear and everything would occupy one and the same plane without distinction. It follows from this that distance is a virtual quality of certain present things, a quality which they only acquire by virtue of an act of the subject. The sound is not distant, I make it distant.

One can make similar reflections on the visual distance of the trees, on the paths which set out in search of the heart of the forest. All this depth of distance exists because of my collaboration, it comes from a structure of

relations which my mind interposes between some sensa-
tions and others. There is, then, a whole portion of
reality which is revealed to us without any effort except
that of opening our eyes and ears—the world of mere
impressions. We may call it the patent world. But there is
also a world beneath it made up of structures of impressions, which if it is latent with relation to the former, is
not less real on that account.[10] We need, it is true, to
open something more than our eyes and to perform more
strenuous acts in order to make this superior world exist
for us, but the measure of this effort neither adds to nor
detracts from the reality of that world. The deep world
is as clear as the superficial one, but it demands more of us.

4

Worlds Beyond

This beneficent forest, which anoints my body with health, has provided a great lesson for my spirit. It is a magisterial forest; old, as teachers should be, serene and complex. In addition it practices the pedagogy of suggestion, the only delicate and profound pedagogy. He who wishes to teach us a truth should not tell it to us, but simply suggest it with a brief gesture, a gesture which starts an ideal trajectory in the air along which we glide until we find ourselves at the feet of the new truth.

Once known, truths acquire a utilitarian crust; they no longer interest us as truths but as useful recipes. That pure, sudden illumination which characterizes truth accompanies the latter only at the moment of discovery. Hence its Greek name *aletheia*, which originally meant the same as the word *apocalipsis* later, that is, discovery, revelation, or rather, unveiling, removing a veil or cover. He who wants to teach us a truth should place us in a position to discover it ourselves.

This forest has taught me that there is a first plane of realities which imposes itself upon me in a violent way; they are the colors, the sounds, the pleasure and the pain of the senses. Towards this plane my attitude is a passive one. But behind those realities there appear others, as the outlines of the higher mountains appear in a sierra when we have reached the first foothills. Some, rising over the tops of others, like new planes of reality, ever more profound, more suggestive, wait for us to ascend them, to reach them. But these higher realities are rather bashful and do not seize us as their victims. On the contrary, they make themselves apparent to us only on one condition: that we desire their existence and that we strive toward them. In a way, then, they depend on our will for their existence. Science, art, justice, manners, religion are orbits of reality which do not overwhelm our persons in a brutal way as hunger or cold does; they exist only for him who wills them to exist.

When the man of great faith says that he sees God in the flowery fields and in the arch of the night sky, he does not express himself more metaphorically than if he should speak of having seen an orange. If there were only a passive way of seeing, the world would be reduced to a chaos of luminous dots; but besides the passive way there is an active seeing which interprets by seeing and sees by interpreting, a seeing which is observing.[11] Plato found a divine word for these visions which come from observing: he called them *ideas*. Just as the third dimension of the orange is only an idea, God is the ultimate dimension of the countryside.

There is no more mysticism in this than when we say we are seeing a faded color. What color do we see when we see a faded color? The blue which we have before us we see *as having been* a more intense blue, and this seeing the present color along with its past color, through what it was formerly, is an active vision which is not like a reflection in a mirror; it is an *idea*. The fading or dulling of a color is a new virtual quality which comes over it, giving it something like a temporal depth. Without the need of reasoning, in a single, momentary vision, we discover the color and its history, its hour of splendor and its present ruin. And something within us echoes, instantly, that same process of decline, of decay; hence the somewhat depressing effect a faded color has on us.

The dimension of depth, whether of space or time,

whether visual or aural, always appears in one surface, so that this surface really possesses two values: one when we take it for what it is materially, the other when we see it in its second virtual life. In the latter case the surface, without ceasing to be flat, expands in depth. This is what we call foreshortening.[12] Vision in depth is made possible by foreshortening, in which we find an extreme case of a fusion of simple vision with a purely intellectual act.

5

The Restoration and Erudition

THE forest opens up its depths around me. A book is in my hand: *Don Quixote,* an ideal forest. Here is another case of depth: that of a book, of this greatest of books. *Don Quixote* is the foreshortening book *par excellence.* There has been a time in Spanish history when people refused to recognize the depth of *Don Quixote.* This period is known by the name of the Restoration.* During that time the heart of Spain slowed down to the lowest number of beats per minute. Let me reproduce here a few words said on another occasion concerning this moment of our collective existence:

"What is the Restoration? According to Cánovas, it is the continuation of the history of Spain. How unfortunate for the history of Spain if the Restoration really represented its legitimate sequence! Luckily it is just the opposite. The Restoration means the interruption of national life. During the first fifty years of the nineteenth century, Spaniards had not shown much complexity, reflection, intellectual maturity, but they had shown courage, exertion, dynamism. If the speeches and books composed in that half century were burnt and replaced by the biographies of their authors, we would gain one hundred per cent. For example, Riego and Narváez as thinkers are, to be sure, a couple of lamentable figures, but as living beings they are two great flashes of energy.

"Toward the year 1854—which is when the Restoration starts beneath the surface—the glowing splendors

* Restoration of the monarchy, 1874–1923. [Translators' note]
70

of that explosion of energy begin to die out upon the sad face of this Spain of ours; the dynamic impulses gradually fall to earth like missiles which have completed their course; Spanish life turns inwards, it becomes the shell of itself. The Restoration consists in living its own hollow life.

"In peoples with a more complete and harmonious spirit than ours, a period of dynamism may be profitably followed by a time of tranquility, calm, and contemplation. The intellect is the means for promoting and organizing peaceful and static interests, like good government, economy, the development of resources and technique. But it has been the characteristic of our people to have excelled in undaunted striving more than in intelligence.

"Spanish life, let us admit it frankly, has been possible until now only as dynamism. When our nation ceases to be dynamic, it falls suddenly into a very deep lethargy, and the only vital function that it exercises is that of dreaming that it is living. Thus it seems as though nothing were lacking in our Restoration. It has great statesmen, great thinkers, great generals, great parties, great equipment, great battles: our army in Tetuan fights against the Moors the same as in the time of Gonzalo de Córdoba; our ships cleave the waves in search of the hostile North as in the time of Philip II; Pereda is another Hurtado de Mendoza, Echegaray is a Calderón reborn. But all this takes place within the orbit of a dream, it is the image of a life in which the only real thing is the act which imagines that life. The Restoration, gentlemen, was a panorama of phantoms, and Cánovas the great impresario of that phantasmagoria." *

How is it possible for a whole people to be satisfied with such false values? The minimum is the measuring

* *Vieja y nueva política*, pp. 22–24. [See *Introduction*, p. 12. Translators' note]

unit in the realm of quantity; in the realm of values, the *highest* values are the measuring unit. Things can only be correctly evaluated by comparing them with the most valuable. In proportion as the really topmost values are suppressed in the perspective of values, those next in line assume this highest rank. The heart of man does not tolerate an absence of the excellent and supreme. As the old proverb says in different words: "In the land of the blind the one-eyed man is king." The ranks are automatically filled by objects and persons less and less fit for them.

During the Restoration the sensitivity for anything really strong, excellent, whole, and profound was lost. The capacity to tremble with awe in the presence of genius passing by was dulled. Nietzsche would have said it was a phase in the perversion of the evaluating instincts. Greatness was no longer felt as great; purity did not move the heart; the quality of perfection and loftiness was invisible like an ultraviolet ray; and inevitably the mediocre and frivolous seemed to become more prevalent. The molehills swelled into mountains and Núñez de Arce passed as a poet.

Let the literary criticism of the period be studied, let Menéndez Pelayo and Valera be read carefully and one will notice this lack of perspective. In good faith those men applauded mediocrity because they had no experience of the profound.* I say experience because talking of genius is not an expression of praise: it is an experiential finding, a phenomenon of religious experience. Schleiermacher finds the essence of the religious in the feeling of dependence pure and simple. When man is

---

* These words do not imply a capricious disdain on my part for these two authors, as this would be inappropriate. They indicate merely a serious defect in their work, one which could coexist with not a few virtues.

absorbed in the contemplation of his inner self, he feels himself to be floating in the universe without any control over himself or anything else; he feels himself depending absolutely on something—let this something be called whatever we wish. So, the healthy mind may be overcome, in the course of reading or of living, by the sensation of an *absolute* superiority—that is, it finds a book, a character whose limits transcend on all sides the orbit of our comprehensive powers. The symptom of the highest values is their boundlessness.*

In these circumstances how could one expect Cervantes to have been placed in the niche to which he is entitled? His divine book was mixed in a very erudite way with our old mystic friars, with our exuberant dramatists, with our lyricists—deserts without flowers.

There is no doubt that the profoundity of *Quixote*, like all profundity, is very far from being obvious. Just as there is a way of seeing which is observing, there is a kind of reading which is *intelligere* or reading what is within, thoughtful reading. The profound meaning of *Quixote* only appears through the latter. But perhaps in a moment of sincerity, all the representative men of the Restoration would have agreed in defining *thinking* with these words: to think is to ask for trouble.

---

* A short time ago—one afternoon in the Spring, while walking over the plain of Extremadura, with a broad landscape of olive trees, dramatized by the solemn flight of some eagles, with the blue outline of the Gata Mountains as background—my good friend, Pío Baroja, tried to convince me that we admire only what we do not understand, that admiration is an effect of lack of understanding. He did not succeed in convincing me, and if he did not succeed, it is unlikely that anyone else will. There is, indeed, incomprehension at the root of the act of admiration, but it is a positive incomprehension: the more we understand of genius, the more there is that remains to be understood.

6

Mediterranean Culture

IMPRESSIONS form a superficial tapestry from which ideal paths seem to lead us toward a deeper reality. Meditation is the mechanism by which we abandon the surfaces, as if they were shores of the mainland, with a feeling of being thrust into a more tenuous element in which there are no material supports. We go forward holding on to ourselves, keeping ourselves in suspension by our own effort within an ethereal orb inhabited by weightless forms. We are accompanied by a keen suspicion that, at the slightest hesitation on our part, all that world would collapse, and we with it. When we meditate, our mind has to be kept at full tension; it is a painful and integral effort. In our meditation we proceed, feeling our way among masses of thoughts, separating some concepts from others, piercing with our glance the imperceptible crevice left between closely related concepts, and having put each concept in its place we stretch out imaginary springs between them so that they will not become confused again. Thus we can come and go comfortably through the landscapes of ideas which present to us their clear and radiant outlines. But some people are incapable of making this effort; people who, having set out to sail in the region of ideas, are attacked by an intellectual vertigo. A confused assemblage of concepts blocks their way. They find no outlet anywhere; they see only a dense confusion around them, a mute and oppressive fog.

When I was a boy, I used to read the books of Menéndez Pelayo with great confidence in his judgment. In these books frequent mention is made of the "Germanic mists," which the author contrasts with the "Latin clarity." On the one hand, I felt highly flattered; on the other hand there arose in me a great sympathy for these poor men of the North, condemned to carry a mist within them. I could not help marveling at the patience with which millions of men, for thousands of years, had been putting up with their wretched lot apparently without complaint and even with some contentment. Later I came to realize that it is simply one of those inaccuracies with which our unfortunate race is being poisoned. There are no such "Germanic mists," and still less such "Latin clarity." These are only words which, if they do mean anything concrete, express a biased misconception.

To be sure, an essential difference between Germanic and Latin culture does exist: the former is the culture of profound realities and the latter the culture of surfaces. They are really, then, two different dimensions of European culture in general, but no difference of clarity exists between them. Nevertheless, before attempting the replacement of the one antithesis, clarity–confusion, by this other, surface–depth, it is necessary to eliminate the source of the error. The error comes from what we should like to understand by the words "Latin culture." It is a golden illusion which stirs within us and with which we French, Italians, and Spaniards like to comfort ourselves in times of decline. We have the weakness of believing ourselves children of the gods. Latinism is a genealogical aqueduct which we erect between our veins and the kidneys of Zeus. Our Latinism is a pretext and a hypocrisy; at bottom we do not care about Rome. The seven hills are the most convenient site from which to behold in the distance the glorious splendor set upon the Aegean Sea, the center of divine radiance: Greece. This is our illusion: we believe ourselves to be heirs to the

Hellenic spirit.

Until fifty years ago it was common to speak of Greeks and Romans without discrimination as the two classic peoples. Since then philology has gone a long way; it has learned to separate delicately the pure and essential from barbarous imitations and mixtures. Each day that passes Greece affirms more emphatically her position *hors ligne* in the history of the world. This privilege rests on perfectly concrete and defined bases: Greece invented the essential themes of European culture, and European culture is the protagonist of history as long as a superior one does not exist. Each new advance in historical research separates Greece further from the Eastern world, reducing the direct influence which the latter was thought to have had upon the Hellenes. On the other hand, the incapacity of the Roman people to invent classic themes is becoming apparent. They did not collaborate with Greece; in fact, they never quite came to understand her. The culture of Rome is, in its higher manifestations, wholly a reflection—a Western Japan. The only thing left to her was the law, the fountainhead of institutions, and now it turns out that she had learned law, too, from Greece.

Once the chain of commonplaces which kept Rome anchored in the Piraeus has been broken, the waves of the Ionian Sea, so famous for their restlessness, have gradually moved her away, leaving her adrift in the Mediterranean, like an intruder thrown out of a house. And now we see that the Romans are only a Mediterranean people. We thus gain a new concept with which to replace the confusing and hypocritical one of a Latin culture: there is no Latin culture, but a Mediterranean culture. For some centuries the history of the world has been confined to the basin of this inland sea. It is a coastal history shared by the peoples living on a narrow strip of land near the

sea from Alexandria to Gibraltar, from Gibraltar to Barcelona, Marseilles, Ostia, Sicily, Crete.* The diffusion of a
specific culture begins perhaps in Rome, and from there it
is transmitted by the divine reverberation of the midday
sun along the seaboard. In the same way, however, it
could have begun at any other point on this coast. Moreover, there was a moment in which fate was on the point
of deciding in favor of another race as the initiator: Carthage. In those magnificent wars—the memory of whose
swords flashing in the blood-stained radiance of the sun
is preserved by our sea in its endless reflections—two
peoples fought, identical in all essentials. The character
of the following centuries would probably not have
changed very much if victory had been transferred from
Rome to Carthage. Both were at the same absolute distance from the Hellenic spirit. Their geographical position was equivalent and the great trade routes would not
have been altered. Their spiritual propensities were also
equivalent; the same ideas had traveled along the same
mental paths. In the depths of our Mediterranean hearts,
Hannibal could take the place of Scipio without our noticing the substitution. It is not surprising then if one
finds similarities between the institutions of the North
African and those of the South European peoples.

Our coasts are daughters of the sea, they belong to it
and live with their backs to the interior. The unity of the
sea is the basis of the identity of the surrounding lands.
The distinction which people have tried to make in the
Mediterranean world, attributing different values to the
Northern and the Southern shores, is an error in historical
perspective. Europe and Africa, as ideas, are like two

* For me the moment when this concept of Mediterranean culture
—that is, non-Latin culture—appeared is the historical problem
raised by the relations between Cretan and Greek culture. Oriental
civilization flows into Crete and another civilization, which is not
Grecian, emerges. So long as Greece is Cretan it is not Hellenic.

enormous centers of conceptual attraction which, in the minds of historians, have reabsorbed their respective coasts. It was not noticed that neither Europe nor Africa existed when Mediterranean culture was a reality. Europe begins when the Germanic peoples enter fully into the unitary organism of the historic world. Africa is born then as the non-Europe, as τὸ ἕτερον vis-à-vis of Europe. Once Italy, France, and Spain were Germanized, Mediterranean culture ceased to be pure and was reduced to be in a greater or lesser degree a Germanic product.

The trade routes began to move from the inland sea and slowly turned towards the mainland of Europe; the thoughts born in Greece turned towards Germania. After a long sleep, Platonic ideas awoke in the minds of Galileo, Descartes, Leibnitz, and Kant, all Germanic. The god of Aeschylus, more ethical than metaphysical, echoed crudely, strongly, in Luther and pure Attic democracy in Rousseau, while the muses of the Parthenon, intact for centuries, yielded one day to Donatello and Michelangelo, Florentine youths of Germanic descent.

7

What a Captain Said to Goethe

WHEN speaking of a specific culture we cannot help thinking of the agent which has produced it—the race. There is no doubt that the diversity of national cultures presupposes, in the last resort, a physiological difference from which it derives in one way or another. But it should be realized that, although the one leads to the other, they are, in fact, two very different problems: that of establishing specific types of historical products—types of science, art, customs, etc.—and, once this has been done, that of searching for the anatomical, or in general, the biological scheme which corresponds to each of them.

We completely lack today the means of establishing causal relations between the races as organic constitutions and as historical modes of being, as intellectual, emotional, artistic, legal, etc., tendencies. We have to content ourselves, and it is no mere trifle, with the merely descriptive operation of classifying historical events or products according to the style or general characteristic which we find manifest in them.

The expression "Mediterranean culture" leaves, then, completely untouched the problem of ethnic kinship between the men who have lived and those who now live on the shores of the inland sea. No matter what their affinity may be, it is a fact that the works of the spirit produced among them have certain peculiarities which distinguish them from Greek and Germanic works. It would be an extremely useful project to attempt a reconstruction of the primary traits, of the basic features, which constitute

79

Mediterranean culture. In doing so it would be well not to mix these elements with what the Germanic inundation has left among peoples who were purely Mediterranean for only a few centuries.

Leaving such an investigation for some philologist gifted with a highly scientific sensibility, I shall limit myself for the moment to one feature commonly accepted as pertaining to so-called Latinism, now reduced to Mediterraneanism, namely clarity. There is no absolute clarity—as the woods have told me in their whispers. Each plane or realm of reality has a clarity of its own. Before regarding clarity as a privilege ascribed to the Mediterranean, it would be timely to ask whether the Mediterranean production is limitless; that is, whether we Southern people have let that domestic brightness of ours illuminate all kinds of things.

The answer is obvious: Mediterranean culture cannot offer products of its own comparable with Germanic science—philosophy, physics, biology. While that culture was still pure, there is no doubt at all that it could not— that is to say, from Alexander to the barbaric invasion. But with what certainty can we speak of Latins or Mediterraneans afterwards? Italy, France, Spain are steeped in Germanic blood. We are essentially mixed races; through our veins flows a tragic physiological contradiction. Houston Chamberlain has been able to speak of the chaotic races.

But leaving aside, as we should, this whole vague ethnic problem, and accepting the ideological output of our countries from the Middle Ages until now as relatively Mediterranean, we find only two ideological high points capable of emulating the magnificent peaks of Germania: Italian Renaissance thought and Descartes. Now, granting that both historical phenomena do not, in their essentials, belong, as I believe, to the Teutonic treasury, we have to recognize in them all the virtues except clarity. Leibnitz, Kant, and Hegel are difficult, but they are as clear as a spring morning; Giordano Bruno and Descartes may not be difficult in the same way but, on the other hand, they are obscure.

If from these heights we descend the slopes of Mediterranean ideology, we discover that it is characteristic of our *Latin* thinkers to have a formal elegance under which lie, if not grotesque combinations of concepts, a radical imprecision, a lack of mental elegance, the sluggishness from which all organisms suffer when they move in an alien element. A very representative figure of the Mediterranean intellect is Juan Bautista Vico. One cannot deny him ideological genius, but anyone who peruses his work learns by experience what chaos means.

Latin clarity, then, is not to be sought after in thought, unless one calls clarity that pedestrian prolixity of French style, that art of *développement* which is taught in the *lycées*.

When Goethe went to Italy he traveled part of the way in the company of an Italian captain. "This captain," Goethe says, "is a true representative of many of his compatriots. Here is a particularly typical trait of his. As I would often remain silent and thoughtful, he said to me once: 'Che pensa! Non deve mai pensar l'uomo, pensando s'invecchia! Non deve fermarsi l'uomo in una sola cosa perchè allora divien matto: *bisogna aver mille cose, una confusione nella testa.*'" *

---

* "What are you thinking about! One ought never to think, thinking ages one! One should never confine oneself to one single thing because he then goes mad: *he needs to have a thousand things, a confusion in his head.*" [Translators' note]

8

The Panther, or on Sensism

THERE is, on the contrary, one trait in the field of plastic arts which really does seem to belong to our culture. "Greek art is confronted in Rome," says Wickhoff, "with a common Latin art based on the Etruscan tradition." * Greek art, which seeks the typical and essential under the concrete appearances, cannot maintain its idealistic effort against the will to imitate reality which from time immemorial had held sway in Rome. Few facts could be more revealing to us than this one. Greek inspiration, notwithstanding its esthetic sufficiency and its authority, breaks down on reaching Italy when it comes up against an artistic instinct of contrary aspiration. The latter is so strong and unmistakable that it does not need to wait for native sculptors to be born to inject itself into Hellenic plastic art. The art patron exercises such spiritual pressures on the Greek artists who have arrived in Rome that the chisel turns aside in their own hands and in place of the latent ideal, it carves what is concrete, apparent, and individual out of the marble block.

Here we have the beginnings of what has since improperly come to be called realism and which really ought to be called impressionism. For twenty centuries the Mediterranean peoples have enrolled their artists under the banner of impressionistic art. Whether exclusively or partially and tacitly, the will to find the sensuous as such has always prevailed. For the Greek what we see is governed and corrected by what we think and only has

* Franz Wickhoff: *Werke*, III, 52–53.

value when it rises to be a symbol of the ideal. For us this ascent is rather a descent: the sensuous breaks its chains as a slave of the idea and declares itself independent. The Mediterranean is an ardent and perpetual justification of sensuousness, of appearances, of surfaces, of the fleeting impressions which things leave on our stimulated nerves.

The same distance that we found between the Mediterranean and the Germanic thinker we find again if we compare a Mediterranean with a Germanic retina. But this time the result of the comparison is in our favor. We Mediterraneans, who do not think clearly, see clearly. If we take away the complicated conceptual framework of philosophical and theological allegory which forms the structure of the *Divine Comedy*, we are left with a few images glistening like precious stones, sometimes imprisoned within the narrow confines of the hendecasyllable, images for which we would give up the rest of the poem. They are simple visions of little moment in which the poet has retained the fleeting nature of a color, of a landscape, of a morning. In Cervantes this power of vision is literally incomparable: it reaches such a point that even without aiming at the description of a thing, the true colors of the thing, its sound, its entire body, will slip now and then into the course of the narrative. Flaubert, referring to *Don Quixote*, said rightly: "Comme on voit ces routes d'Espagne qui ne sont nulle part décrites!" *

If we move from a page of Cervantes to one of Goethe's—before and independently of any comparisons between the value of the worlds created by the two poets —we perceive a radical difference: Goethe's world is not presented before us in an immediate way. Things and persons float about, always at a set distance, as if visualized in the memory or in a dream.

When a thing possesses all that is needed to be what

* *Correspondance,* II, 305.

it is, it still lacks a decisive quality: appearance, actuality. The famous sentence in which Kant attacks the metaphysics of Descartes—"thirty possible *thaler* are not less than thirty actual *thaler*"—may be philosophically exact, but in any case it contains a candid confession of the limits peculiar to Germanism. For a Mediterranean person the important thing is not the essence of an object but its presence, its actuality. We prefer the vivid sensation of things to the things themselves. The Latins have called this realism. But "realism" being a Latin concept and not a Latin vision, it is a term which inevitably lacks clarity. To what things—*res*—does that realism refer? As long as we do not distinguish between things and the appearance of things, what is most genuine in Southern art will escape our understanding.

Goethe also looks for things, as he himself says: "The organ with which I have understood the world is the eye"; * and Emerson adds: "Goethe sees at every pore." Within his Germanic limitation, Goethe may perhaps be considered to have a visual mind, a temperament for which the apparent exists. But, compared to our artists of the South, this seeing of Goethe is rather a thinking with the eyes.

Nos oculos eruditos habemos: ** what in seeing belongs to mere impression is incomparably more energetic in the Mediterranean and for this reason people here find it usually sufficient. The pleasure of seeing, of examining, of sensing the surface of things by the pupil is the distinguishing feature of our art. It should not be called realism because it does not consist in the emphasis on the *res*, on the things, but on the *appearance* of things. It would be better to call it "apparentism," illusionism, impressionism.

* *Dichtung und Wahrheit*, VI.
** Cicero, *Paradox.*

The Greeks were realists indeed, but realists of remembered things. Reminiscence, by holding objects aloof, purifies and idealizes them, removing from them particularly that harsh quality which even the sweetest and softest possess when they act directly on our senses. And the Mediterranean art which began in Rome—and which could have come from Carthage, Marseilles, or Malaga— seeks precisely that harsh fierceness of the actual as such. One day in the first century B.C., the news spread through Rome that Pasiteles, the great sculptor of the type that appeals to us, had been devoured by a panther which he was using as a model. He may be called the first martyr, for Mediterranean clarity too has its own martyrs. The name of Pasiteles, martyr of sensism, can certainly be inscribed in the list of our cultural saints.

Sensism, in short, is what we ought to call this aptitude attributed to our inland sea. We are mere supports for the organs of the senses: we see, hear, smell, touch, taste, we feel organic pleasure and pain. With a certain pride we repeat Gautier's expression: "the external world exists for us." The external world! But is not the imperceptible world—the deeper zones—also external to the ego? There is no doubt that it is external and it is so in a very high degree. The only difference lies in the fact that "reality" —the wild beast, the panther—falls upon us in a violent way, breaking in upon us through the breaches of the senses, while ideality only yields to our effort. Our danger is that, invaded by the external, we may be driven out of ourselves, left with our inner selves empty, and thus become transformed into gateways on the highway through which a throng of objects come and go.

The predominance of the senses usually implies a deficiency in inner powers. What is meditating as compared with seeing? As soon as our retina is hit by the arrow from without, our inner personal energy hastens up and stops the intrusion. The impression is registered, subjected to civilized order, it is *thought*, and in this way it is integrated in the building-up of our personality and co-operates within it.

9

Things and Their Meaning

ALL this notorious controversy between Germanic mists and Latin clarity settles down with the recognition of two kinds of men: the meditative and the sensuous. For the latter the world is a reverberating surface; their realm is the radiant face of the universe—*facies totius mundi,* as Spinoza said. The meditative type, on the contrary, lives in the dimension of depth. Just as the organ of the sensuous man is the retina, the palate, the tips of the fingers, etc., the organ of the thinker is the concept. The concept is the normal organ of depth.

Heretofore I have fixed my attention chiefly on temporal depth, which is the past, and spacial depth, which is distance. But both are only examples, special cases of depth. What does depth consist of, taken *in genere?* It was already alluded to when I contrasted the patent world of mere impressions with the latent worlds made up of structures of impressions. A structure is a reality in a secondary sense; I mean, it is a group of things or simple material elements, plus the order in which these elements are arranged.[13] It is evident that the reality of that order has a value or significance different from the reality possessed by its elements. This ash tree is green and is on my right: being green and being on my right are qualities which it possesses, but their possession does not mean the same with respect to each of them. When the sun sinks behind these hills I shall follow one of the ill-defined paths opened like imaginary furrows in the tall grass. On my way I shall cut the little yellow flowers which grow here as in a primitive painting, and going towards the Monastery, I shall leave the solitary wood while in the background the cuckoo lets fall its impertinent evening song on the landscape. Then this ash tree will go on being green, but it will have been deprived of the other quality: it will no longer be on my right. Colors are material qualities; right and left, relative qualities which things possess only in relation to other things. It is this interlocking of things that forms a structure.

How unimportant a thing would be if it were only what it is in isolation? How poor, how barren, how blurred! One might say that there is in each thing a certain latent potentiality to be many other things, which is set free and expands when other things come into contact with it. One might say that each thing is fertilized by the others; that they desire each other as male and female; that they love each other and aspire to unite, to collect in communities, in organisms, in structures, in worlds. What we call "nature" is only the maximum structure into which all material elements have entered, and nature is a work of love because it means the generation or creation of some things inside others, the birth of one from another in which it was preconceived, pre-formed, virtually contained.

When we open our eyes—as we have observed—there is a first moment in which objects rush frantically into our visual range. It seems as though they expand, stretch, and break up like a gaseous mass torn by a gust of wind. But gradually order sets in. First the things which fall in the center of vision settle down into focus, followed by those which occupy the borders. This settling down and focusing of the outlines results from our attention, which has put them in order, that is to say, has spread a net of relationships between them. A thing cannot be focused or confined except with others. If we continue paying attention to one object, it will become more clearly perceived because we shall keep finding in it more reflections of and connections with the surrounding things. The ideal would be to make each thing the center of the universe. And this is what the depth of something means: what there is in it of reflection of other things, allusion to other things. The reflection is the most apparent form in which one thing virtually exists in another. The "meaning" of a thing is the highest form of its coexistence with other things—it is its depth dimension. No, it is not enough for me to have the material body of a thing; I need, besides, to know its "meaning," that is to say, the mystic shadow which the rest of the universe casts on it.

Let us ask ourselves about the meaning of things or, in other words, let us make of each thing the virtual center of the world. But isn't this what love does? Is it not one and the same thing to say that we love an object and that it is for us the center of the universe, the place where all the threads forming the web of our life, of our world, come together? Of course it is. It is an old and venerable doctrine. Plato sees in "*eros*" an impetus which leads to the interlocking of things; it is, he says, a unitive force and is the passion of synthesis. Hence, in his opinion, philosophy, which searches for the meaning of things, is driven by "*eros*." Meditation is an erotic exercise: the concept, an amorous rite.

It may seem strange to associate the philosophical sensibility with the muscular restlessness and the sudden rush of the blood we feel when an attractive young woman, heels tapping, passes close by. It may be strange and ambiguous and dangerous, both for philosophy and for our relations with women. But, perhaps Nietzsche is right when he shouts to us: "Live dangerously!" Let us leave the question for another occasion.* Now we should note that if the impression of a thing conveys to us its matter, its body, the concept contains all that the thing is in relation with other things, all that superior treasure with which the object is enriched when it becomes part of a structure.

The content of the concept is found in what there is between things. But, first of all, there are limits between things. Have we ever asked ourselves where the limits of an object are? Are they within the object? Obviously not. If there only were a single, isolated object, it would be limitless. One object ends where another begins. Would it be, then, that the limit of one thing is another thing? It is not that either, because this other thing needs, in its turn, to be limited by the first. Where are the limits, then?

Hegel writes that the thing is not where its limit is. According to this, the limits are like virtual new things which interpolate and interject themselves between the actual things, schematic natures whose purpose is to mark the borders of beings, to bring them closer together so that they may coexist and, at the same time, to separate them so that they do not merge together and annihilate one another. The concept is just this—no more, but no less, either. Thanks to it, things respect one another and can come together without encroaching upon one another.[14]

* Concerning these relationships between thought, attention and love, and also the distance between love and the sexual impulse, see my book *Meditación de Don Juan* [Introducción a un "Don Juan," *O.C.*, VI, 121-137] and *El Espectador*, vols. I and II [*O.C.*, II.] [In the first edition of the *Meditaciones* (1914), Ortega referred here to a book in preparation, *La estética de "Mío Cid*," Chapter VI, "Diálogo del amor a orillas del Duero," which he never published. Translators' note]

10

The Concept

THE UTMOST clarity in this matter of the mission of the
concept is important to anyone who loves the Spain
of the future honestly and deeply. At first glance, it
is true, such a question seems to be too academic to
be treated as a national issue. But without renouncing
our first glance at a question, why should we not aspire to take a second and a third glance? It is opportune, then, for us to ask this question: when, in addition to seeing something, we have a concept of it, what
does this concept convey to us over and above that vision? What do we gain by the concept of the forest which
is added to our feeling of being mysteriously embraced
by the forest around us? First of all, the concept appears
to us as a repetition or reproduction of the thing itself,
cast in a spectral substance. We are thinking of what the
Egyptians used to call the *double* of each being, the
shadowy replica of an organism. Compared with the
thing itself, the concept is only a specter or even less
than a specter. Therefore no one in his right senses would
ever think of exchanging his fortune in things for a
fortune in specters. The concept cannot be considered
a kind of new subtle thing destined to take the place of
material things. The mission of the concept, then, is not
to displace the intuition, the real impression. Reason cannot and should not aim at replacing life. This very opposition between reason and life, so much used today by
those who do not want to work, is in itself upon to suspicion. As if reason were not a vital and spontaneous

function, of the same kind as seeing or touching! [15]

Let us go on a little further. What gives the concept that spectral character is its schematic content. The concept retains merely the outline of the object. Now, in a scheme, we possess only the limits of the object, the outline which encloses the matter, the real substance of the object. These limits, as has been indicated, mean only the relationship in which any object finds itself with respect to all other objects. If we take one piece out of a mosaic we have the outline of the piece left in the form of a hollow, limited by the surrounding pieces. In the same way the concept expresses the ideal place, the ideal hollow corresponding to each object within the system of realities. Without the concept we would not be certain where an object begins or ends, for the objects as impressions are volatile and fleeting, they slip out of our hands; we do not possess them. When the concept ties some of them together, it fixes them and delivers them to us as captives. Plato says that impressions escape us if we do not secure them with our reason, as the statues of Demetrius, according to the legend, used to flee from the gardens at night if they were not tied.

The concept will never convey to us what the impression does, that is, the body of things. However, this is not due to any deficiency in the concept, but to the fact that the concept does not claim such a function. The impression will never convey to us what the concept does, namely, the form, the physical and moral sense of things. So that if we restore to the word *perception* its etymological meaning—which refers to "catching, taking captive"—the concept will be the real instrument or organ for the perception and apprehension of things. It fulfills its mission and its essence, then, not by being a new thing, but an organ or apparatus for the possession of things.

We feel nowadays very far from Hegel's dogma, which sees in thought the ultimate substance of all reality. The world is too wide and too rich for thought to assume the responsibility for all that occurs in the world. But on dethroning reason, let us take care to put it in its place. Not everything is thought, but without thought we do not possess anything fully.* This is what the concept has to offer us beyond the mere impression: each concept is literally an organ by means of which we capture things. Vision becomes complete only through the concept. Sensation gives us only the shapeless and pliable matter of each object; it gives us the impression of things, not the things themselves.

* Concerning some aspects of the relations between reason and life, see the *Meditación de Don Juan* [Introducción a un "Don Juan," *O.C.*, VI 121–137], and especially *El tema de nuestro tiempo* [*The Modern Theme*, trans. J. Cleugh, New York, 1933]. [This note did not appear in the 1914 edition. Translators' note]

11

Culture—Security

ONLY when something has been thought does it come within our power. Only when elementary things are subdued can we advance toward the more complex. Every advance made in the control and expansion of moral territories presupposes the peaceful, definitive possession of others on which we stand. If nothing is secure beneath our feet, all our higher achievements will fail. For this reason an impressionistic culture is condemned to be a nonprogressive culture. It will exist in a discontinuous way; it will be able to offer great figures and isolated works throughout its existence, but all kept on the same level. Every impressionist of genius re-creates his world out of nothing, not from where another predecessor of genius left it.

Has this not been the case in the history of Spanish culture? Every Spanish genius has started all over again from chaos as if nothing had existed before. It is undeniable that this is the reason for the rough, original, and harsh character of our great artists and men of action. It would be inconceivable and foolish to ignore this quality, as foolish as to think that this quality is enough, that there are no other virtues.

Our great men are characterized by an Adam psychology. Goya is an Adam—a first man. If one changed the costumes and the externals of a technique which sums up the greatest delicacies of eighteenth-century Anglo-French art, the spirit of his paintings could be transferred to the tenth century A.D. and even to the tenth century

B.C. Shut up in the cave of Altamira, Goya would have been the painter of the *uri* or wild bulls. A man without age or history, Goya represents—as does Spain perhaps—a paradoxical form of culture: wild culture, culture without a yesterday, without progression, without security; a culture in perpetual struggle with elemental forces, disputing every day the possession of the land which it occupies; in short, a frontier culture.*

These words should not be taken in an estimative sense. I do not mean to say now that Spanish culture is worth more or less than any other culture. It is not a question of evaluating, but of understanding the Spanish spirit. Let us abandon the inane dithyrambic attitude assumed by our scholars when they dealt with Spanish deeds. Let us try our formulas of understanding and intelligence; let us not judge or appraise. Only thus can the affirmation of the essentially Spanish become fruitful some day.

The Goya case illustrates perfectly what I am now trying to say. Our emotion—I refer to the emotion of those who are capable of sincere and deep emotions—is perhaps strong and poignant when we look at his paintings, but it is not predictable. One day it carries us away in its feverish dynamism and another day it irritates us with its capriciousness and senselessness. What the merciless Aragonese pours into our hearts is always problematical. It might well be that his indocility is the symptom of all that is definitely great, or it might be just the opposite. But it is a fact that the best products of our culture contain an ambiguity, a peculiar uncertainty.

On the other hand, the preoccupation which, like a new tremor, begins to rise in the breasts of the Greeks and

* [In a footnote to his 1914 edition, Ortega referred again to *La estética de "Mío Cid"* for an exposition of this idea and an essay on the culture of Spain interpreted as a frontier culture. Translators' note]

spreads later to other peoples of the European continent, is the anxiety for security, for certainty—τὸ ἀσφαλές—* Culture for the dark-eyed men who meditate, argue, sing, preach, and dream in Ionia, Attica, Sicily, and Magna Graecia, means what is firm as opposed to what is unstable, what is fixed as opposed to what is fleeting, what is clear as opposed to what is obscure. Culture is not the whole of life, but only the moment of security, of certainty, of clarity. And the Greeks invent the concept as an instrument, not for replacing the spontaneity of life, but for making it secure.[16]

* Plato, *Phaedo,* 100 D, 101 D.

12

Light as an Imperative

ONCE the purpose of the concept has been reduced to its true proportions and it is realized that it can never convey to us the live substance of the universe, I do not run the risk of seeming too intellectualistic if I qualify slightly the preceding remarks about the various kinds of clarity. The peculiar way in which surfaces are clear is certainly different from that in which deep things are clear. There is a clarity of impression and a clarity of meditation. However, since the question is presented in a controversial tone, the assumption of Latin clarity precluding the existence of Germanic clarity, I must say all that I think about the subject.

My thought—and not only my thought!—tends to combine all my ancestral heritage in one firm integration. My soul comes from known parents: I am not Mediterranean only. I am not willing to confine myself within the Iberian corner of myself. I need all my ancestry so that my heart may not feel miserable. I need my whole ancestry and not only the golden beams which the sun sheds upon the elongated turquoise expanse of our sea. My eyes transmit bright visions to my soul; but from the depths of these visions potent meditations also arise. Who has put in my heart these resounding reminiscences in which the intimate voices of the wind from the depths of the Germanic forests still echo like the sounds of the ocean in a seashell? Why does the Spaniard persist in living anachronistically within himself? Why does he forget his Germanic inheritance? Without it, let there be no doubt about it, he would suffer an ambiguous destiny. Behind his Mediterranean features there seems to lurk the Asiatic or African gesture, and in the latter—in the Asiatic or African eyes and lips—lies the subhuman animal, as if only dozing, ready to invade the whole face. And there is in me a substantial, cosmic aspiration to raise myself from the wild beast as from a bloodstained bed. Do not force me to be only a Spaniard if by Spaniard is meant only a man of the sun-drenched coast. Do not introduce civil wars into my heart; do not incite the Iberian within me with his harsh, wild passions, against the blonde man of Germanic heritage, meditative and sentimental, who breathes in the twilight zone of my soul. I try to make peace among my inner personalities and I urge them toward collaboration. For this a hierarchy is necessary, and one of the two types of clarity must be made pre-eminent.

Clarity means peaceful spiritual possession, sufficient domination of our mind over images, not to suffer anxiety about the threat that the object grasped will flee from us. Now, this clarity is conveyed to us by the concept. This clarity, this certainty, this fullness of possession, are felt in European works and are usually absent in Spanish art, science, or politics. All cultural endeavor is an interpretation—elucidation, explanation or exegesis—of life. Life is the eternal text, the burning bush by the edge of the path from which God speaks. Culture—art or science or politics—is the commentary, it is that aspect of life in which, by an act of self-reflection, life acquires polish and order. That is why the work of culture can never retain the problematic character pertaining to all that is merely living. In order to master the unruly torrent of life the learned man meditates, the poet quivers, and the political hero erects the fortress of his will. It would be odd indeed if the result of all these efforts led only to duplicating the problem of the universe. No, man has a mission of clarity upon earth. This mission has not been revealed to

him by God nor is it imposed on him from without by
anyone or anything. He carries it within him, it is the very
root of his constitution.[17] Within his breast arises per-
petually a tremendous ambition for clarity—as Goethe,
taking his place in the row of highest human peaks,
sang:

> I declare myself of the family of those
> Who from obscurity to clarity aspire.

When he is about to die, in the middle of an early spring
day, his final words utter a last desire, the last shaft of the
exemplary old archer: *Light, more light!*

Clarity is not life, but it is the fullness of life. How is
it to be attained without the help of the concept? The
concept is clarity within life, the light shed on things;
nothing more, nothing less. Each new concept is a new
organ which opens within us upon a portion of the world
which was silent and invisible before. He who gives us an
idea increases our life and expands reality around us. The
Platonic notion that we do not look with our eyes but
through or by means of our eyes is literally true: we
observe by means of concepts.* *Idea* in Plato meant point
of view.

Faced with the problematic character of life, culture—
in so far as it is living and authentic—represents a treasury
of principles. We can argue about the principles best
suited to solve that problem, but whatever they may be,
they must be principles; and a principle, to be a principle,
must begin by not being a problem. This is the difficulty
with which religion is faced and which has always kept it
at variance with other forms of human culture, especially
with reason. The religious spirit links the mystery of life
with still darker and higher mysteries, whereas life appears to us to be a problem potentially solvable or, at least
not unsolvable *a limine.*

* See the dialogue *Theaetetus.*

13

Integration

THE WORK of art, no less than the other manifestations of the spirit, has this elucidating or, we might say, *Luciferian* mission. An artistic style which does not contain the key to its own interpretation, which consists of a mere reaction of one part of life—the individual heart—to the rest of it, will produce only ambiguous values. Great styles have a sort of stellar or lofty mountain atmosphere through which the refracted life comes forth subdued and purified, drenched in clarity. The artist has not limited himself to producing verses as an almond-tree bursts into bloom in March; he has risen above himself, above his vital spontaneity; he has soared above his own heart and above his surroundings, circling about like the eagle in majestic flight. Through his rhythms, his harmonies of color and line, his perceptions and sentiments, we discover in him a strong power of reflection, of meditation. In the most diverse forms, every great style contains a meridian refulgence and it is like the serenity that descends upon the stormy elements.

This is what our traditionally Spanish productions have lacked. We find ourselves facing them as we face life itself. Some claim that herein lies their great virtue. I reply that herein lies their great defect. As far as life, spontaneity, sorrow and darkness are concerned, I have enough with my own, with those which flow through my veins; I have enough with my own flesh and my own bones and the flameless fire of my conscience above my flesh and bones. What I need now is clarity, a dawn above my life. But these traditional works are merely an enlargement of my own flesh and bones, a horrible conflagration which reproduces the one that is in my spirit. They are like me, and I am searching for something which may be more than I—more of a certainty than I.

On the moral map of Europe we Spaniards represent the extreme predominance of impressions. Concepts have never been our forte. There is no doubt that we should be unfaithful to our destiny if we should abandon the energetic affirmation of impressionism lying in our past. I not propose abandonment, but the opposite: an integration. Genuine tradition cannot be, in its best sense, anything but a supporting ground for individual vacillation—a *terra firma* for the spirit. This, our culture can never be if it does not base and organize its sensism upon the cultivation of meditation.

The case of *Quixote* is truly representative in this as in all respects. Can there be a more profound book than this humble novel with its burlesque tone? And, yet, what is *Quixote?* Do we know exactly what it tries to suggest to us about life? The brief illuminations which have fallen upon it come from foreign spirits: Schelling, Heine, Turgenev, etc. They are momentary and insufficient elucidations. For those men *Quixote* was a divine curiosity; it was not, as it is for us, the problem of their destiny.

Let us be sincere: *Quixote* is an ambiguity. All the praise bestowed by our national eloquence has been of no avail. All the learned research into the life of Cervantes has not cleared up even one corner of this colossal ambiguity. Is Cervantes making fun of something? And of what? Far away, alone in the open Manchegan plain, the lanky figure of Don Quixote bends like an interrogation mark, like a guardian of the Spanish secret, of the ambiguity of Spanish culture. What was that poor taxgatherer mocking from the depths of a dungeon? And precisely what is mocking? Is mockery necessarily a negation?

There is no book more potent in symbolic allusions to the universal meaning of life, and, yet, there is no book in which we find fewer anticipations, fewer clues for its own interpretation. For this reason Shakespeare would appear to be a thinker as compared with Cervantes. Shakespeare never fails to give us a sort of meditative counterpoint, a subtle row of concepts on which our understanding rests.

A few words from Hebbel, the great German dramatist of the past century, clarify what I am now trying to say: "I have usually been aware of a certain sediment of ideas in my works; I have been accused of building my works upon them, but this is not true. That basis of ideas must be understood as a chain of mountains which shuts out the landscape." I believe that there is something like this in Shakespeare: a row of concepts inserted during the last phase of his inspiration, like very delicate tracings which guide our eyes while we pass through the fantastic forest of his poetry. In a greater or lesser degree Shakespeare always explains himself.

Does this happen in the case of Cervantes? When one calls him a realist, does not that possibly indicate one's desire to point out his retention of pure impressions and his avoidance of any general and ideological formula? Is not this, perhaps, the supreme gift of Cervantes? At least, it is doubtful that there are other truly profound Spanish books. All the more reason for us to focus on *Quixote*, our great question: O God, what is Spain? What is this Spain, this spiritual promontory of Europe, this thing we may call the prow of the continental soul in the broad expanse of the globe, in the midst of innumerable races, lost in a limitless yesterday and an endless tomorrow, below the immense and cosmic cold of the twinkling stars?

Where is there a clear word, a single radiant word which can satisfy an honest heart and a sensitive mind, a word which can throw light on the destiny of Spain? Woe to the race which does not stop at the crossroads before continuing on its way, which does not make a problem out of its own inner life, which does not feel the heroic necessity of justifying its destiny and of throwing light on its mission in history! The individual cannot get his bearings in the universe except through his race, because he is immersed in it like the drop of water in the passing cloud.

14

Parable

PEARY relates that on his polar trip he traveled one whole day toward the North, making his sleigh dogs run briskly. At night he checked his bearings to determine his latitude and noticed with great surprise that he was much further South than in the morning. He had been toiling all day toward the North on an immense iceberg drawn southward by an ocean current.

15

Criticism as Patriotism

A PROBLEM is not a problem unless it contains a real contradiction. Nothing is so important for us today, in my opinion, as to sharpen our sensitivity to the problem of Spanish culture, that is, to feel Spain as a contradiction. Those who are incapable of this, or do not perceive the underlying ambiguity beneath our feet, will be of little use to us.

It is necessary for our meditation to penetrate as far as the last layer of our ethnic consciousness, to analyze its finest sinews, to revise all the national suppositions without accepting any of them superstitiously.

It is said that all of the purely Greek blood that remains in the world today could be put in a wineglass. It must be difficult, therefore, to find a drop of pure Hellenic blood, but I believe it is much more difficult to find true Spaniards either today or in the past. There is perhaps no other species with fewer specimens. There are, it is true, those who think otherwise. The discrepancy arises from the fact that the word "Spanish," used so frequently, runs the risk of not being understood in its full sense. We forget that, in the last analysis, each race is an experiment in a new way of living, in a new sensibility. When a race succeeds in developing its particular energies fully, the earth is enriched in an incalculable way: the new sensibility promotes new uses and institutions, new architecture and new poetry, new sciences and new aspirations, new sentiments and new religion. On the contrary, when a race fails, all this possible innovation and accretion remain irrevocably unborn because the sensibility which creates them is not transferable. A people is a way of life and, as such, consists of a certain simple and differential modulation which gradually organizes the surrounding matter. Occasionally, external causes may turn aside from its ideal course this movement of creative organization in which the way of life of a people is developing, and the result is the most monstrous and lamentable that can be imagined. Each step forward in that diversionary process buries more deeply the original intention, gradually encasing it in the lifeless crust of abortive, faulty and inferior products. That people becomes every day less and less what it was meant to be.

Since this is the case with Spain, we must consider as perverse a patriotism without perspective or hierarchies, which accepts as Spanish all that happens to have been produced in our land and confuses the most inept degeneration with what is essential to Spain. Is it not a cruel sarcasm that after three and a half centuries of misguided wandering, we are asked to follow the national tradition? Tradition! The traditional reality in Spain has actually consisted in the gradual annihilation of Spain as a possibility. No, we cannot follow tradition. To be Spanish means for me a very lofty promise which has been fulfilled only in extremely rare cases. No, we cannot follow tradition; on the contrary, we must go against tradition, beyond tradition. From the traditional débris we must save the primary substance of the race, the Hispanic core, the simple Spanish tremor before chaos. What is usually called Spain is not that, but actually the failure of all that. In one huge painful bonfire we ought to burn the inert traditional mask, the Spain that has been and then, among the well-sifted ashes, we shall find the iridescent gemlike Spain that could have been.

For this, we shall have to free ourselves from the superstition of the past, lest we be seduced by it as if Spain were confined to her past. The Mediterranean sailors found out that there was only one means of guarding against the fatal song sung by the sirens, and that was to sing it backwards. Likewise those who today love the things Spain might be, have to sing the historical legend of Spain backwards, so as to get across it to the half-dozen places where the poor heart of our race throbs with purity and intensity.

One of these essential experiences, the greatest perhaps, is Cervantes. Here is a Spanish plenitude. Here is a word which we can brandish on every occasion as if it were a lance. Alas! If we only knew with certainty the secret of Cervantes' style, of his manner of approaching things, we would have found out everything, because on these spiritual heights there reigns such indestructible solidarity that a poetic style brings with it philosophical, moral, scientific, and political conceptions. If one day someone were to come and reveal to us the profile of Cervantes' style, it would suffice for us to prolong its lines over our other collective problems and we would awake to a new life. Then, if there is courage and genius amongst us, the new Spanish experiment could be made in its purest form. But until that someone arrives, let us be content with vague indications, more fervent than exact, and try to keep our respectful distance from the great novelist, lest we say something improper or extravagant in our effort to come too close to him. In my opinion, that is what happened a few years ago to the most famous teacher of Spanish literature, when he tried to sum up Cervantes by saying that his characteristic was . . . his good sense. There is nothing so dangerous as treating a demigod too familiarly—even though he may be a tax-collecting demigod.

Such were the thoughts that came to me during a spring

afternoon in the wood that surrounds the Monastery of the Escorial, our great poem in stone. They prompted my decision to write these essays on *Quixote*.

The twilight blue had settled over the whole landscape. The birds' voices lay dormant in their tiny throats. When I went away from the stream, I entered a zone of absolute silence; my heart then emerged from the depth of things like an actor who steps forward on the stage to say the last dramatic words. Thump, thump . . . The rhythmic beating began and a terrestrial emotion pervaded my soul. A star on high was keeping time with its twinkling, as if it were a sidereal heart, a twin brother of mine, and like my own, filled with wonder and tenderness by the marvel of the world.

First Meditation

First Meditation

A SHORT TREATISE ON THE NOVEL

LET us consider briefly the aspect of *Quixote* which seems most external. It is said to be a novel; it is also said, and perhaps rightly, that it is the first novel in point of time and in merit. Much of the satisfaction that the contemporary reader finds in it comes from what it has in common with the kind of literature favored in our times. As we peruse its old pages, we find in them a modern note which is bound to draw the venerable book closer to our hearts: we feel it to be at least as close to our innermost sensibility as are the builders of the contemporary novel —Balzac, Dickens, Flaubert, or Dostoievski.

But what is a novel? Perhaps it is not the fashion to discuss the essence of literary genres. The subject is considered to be a rhetorical one. There are those who even deny the existence of literary genres. Nevertheless, those of us who flee from fashions and resolve to live among the hurrying throng with the calm of a pharaoh may ask ourselves: what is a novel?

1

Literary Genres

THE old poetics understood by literary genres certain rules of craftsmanship which the poet was to follow, empty patterns, formal structures, within which the muse, like a docile bee, deposited its honey. I am not speaking of literary genres in this sense. The form and content are inseparable and the poetic content flows on freely without the constriction of abstract rules. Nevertheless, one must distinguish between content and form: they are not the same thing. Flaubert used to say that the form comes out of the content as heat does from fire. The metaphor is accurate, but it would be still more accurate to say that the form is the organ and the content the function which creates it. Literary genres are, then, the poetic functions, the directions, in which esthetic creation moves.

The modern tendency to deny the difference between the content or theme and its form or expressive apparatus seems to me as trivial as its Scholastic differentiation. Really, the difference is the same as that which exists between a direction and a road. To take a direction is not the same thing as to have gone all the way to our destination. The stone which is thrown carries within it already the curve of its flight. This curve becomes, so to speak, the explanation, development and fulfillment of the original impulse. Thus tragedy is the expansion of a certain fundamental poetic theme and of nothing else; it is the expansion of the tragic element. The form therefore contains the same thing that was in the content, but it presents in a clear, articulated, developed way what in the content was only a tendency or mere intention. Hence the inseparability of content and form as the two distinct moments in the creation of the same thing.

Contrary to the old poetics I understand, then, by literary genres, certain basic themes, mutually exclusive, true esthetic categories. The epic, for example, is not the name of a poetic form but of a basic poetic content which reaches fulfillment in the process of its expansion or manifestation. Lyric poetry is not a conventional idiom into which may be translated what has already been said in a dramatic or novelistic idiom, but at one and the same time a certain thing to be said and the only way to say it fully.

In one way or another man is always the essential theme of art,[18] and the genres understood as mutually exclusive esthetic themes, equally essential and final, are wide vistas seen from the main sides of human nature. Each epoch brings with it a basic interpretation of man. Or rather, the epoch does not bring the interpretation with it but actually *is* such an interpretation. For this reason, each epoch prefers a particular genre.

2

Exemplary Novels

DURING the second half of the nineteenth century the people of Europe enjoyed reading novels. There is no doubt that when the passage of time has sifted out the innumerable facts which made up that period, the triumph of the novel will remain as an outstanding and representative phenomenon. Nevertheless, is it clear what the word *novel* means? Cervantes called certain of his less important productions *exemplary novels*, but is the meaning of this title so simple?

The use of *exemplary* is not so strange: that tinge of morality which even the most profane of Spanish authors gives to his stories, belongs to the heroic hypocrisy practiced by the best men of the seventeenth century. This century, when the great spiritual seed of the Renaissance yields its golden harvest, does not find any difficulty in accepting the Counter-Reformation and turns to the Jesuit colleges. It is the century when Galileo, after inaugurating the new physics, does not object to contradicting himself when the Church of Rome sets its harsh dogmatic hand upon him. It is the century when Descartes, having scarcely discovered the principle of his method, which is going to turn theology into *ancilla philosophiae* rushes to Loreto to thank Our Lady for his fortunate discovery. But this century of Catholic triumphs is not so unpropitious a time as to prevent the great rationalistic systems from making their first appearance as formidable fortresses against faith. Let this be borne in mind by those who, with enviable simplicity, lay all the blame on the Inquisition for the poverty of thought in Spain.

But let us get back to the title of "novels" which Cervantes gives to his collection. I find here two very different types of composition, although I do not deny that something of the spirit of each may be found in the other. The important thing is that a radically different artistic intention prevails in each series, that poetic creation moves towards a different point in each. How is it possible to include in one and the same genre, on the one hand *The Liberal Lover*, *The Spanish-English Lady*, *The Force of Blood*, *The Two Damsels*, and on the other *Rinconete and Cortadillo* and *The Jealous Estremaduran?* Let us indicate the difference in a few words: in the first series we are told stories of love and fortune. They are about children, who, torn from the family tree, are subjected to unexpected adventures; about young men who, swept along by an erotic whirlwind, flash dizzily across the horizon like shooting stars; about worn-out, wandering young ladies who sigh deeply in the rooms of inns and speak of their maltreated virginity in Ciceronian style. Sometimes, in one such inn, three or four of these red-hot threads, spun by chance and passion, entangle various pairs of hearts together. To the great amazement of the people at the inn, the most extraordinary recognitions and coincidences then follow. All that is related to us in these novels is improbable, and the interest which it awakens in us springs from its very unlikeliness. The *Persiles*, which is like a long exemplary novel of this kind, reassures us that Cervantes deliberately sought such improbability. The fact that he should close his cycle of creation with this book cautions us not to simplify things too much.

The stories told by Cervantes in some of his novels are the same venerable stories invented by the Aryan imag-

ination many, many centuries ago; so many centuries ago
that we can find them already suggested in the original
myths of Greece and the Near East. Should one apply
the name *novel* to the literary genre which takes in this
first series of Cervantes' novels? There is no objection,
but one should specify that this literary genre consists in
the narration of improbable, fanciful, unreal events.

Something very different seems to be attempted in the
other series, of which *Rinconete and Cortadillo* can be
taken as representative. Here scarcely anything happens;
our minds are not excited by dynamic outbursts of passion nor do they hurry from one paragraph to the next
in order to discover the turn of events. If one takes a
step forward it is to rest again and look all around. What
is sought is a series of static and detailed views. The characters and their actions are so far from being unusual and
unbelievable as to be actually uninteresting. No one can
say, for example, that the young rogues Rincón and
Cortado, or the "shady dames" Gananciosa and Cariharta,
or the ruffian Repolido, possess any attraction in themselves. As we go on reading, in fact, we realize that it is
not they themselves but the presentation of them given
us by the author which succeeds in gaining our interest.
Moreover, if they were not indifferent characters to us
because they are so well-known and commonplace, the
work would lead our esthetic emotion along very different paths. The insignificance, the ordinariness, the verisimilitude of these creatures are essential here.

The contrast with the artistic intention of the previous
series could not be greater. There it was the characters
themselves and their adventures which were the cause of
the esthetic enjoyment. The writer could reduce his own
intervention to the minimum. Here, on the contrary, we
are only interested in the way in which the author reflects
on his retina the vulgar countenances of which he speaks.

Cervantes realized this difference clearly when he wrote in the *Colloquy of the Dogs:*

There is one thing which I should like to point out to you, and you will see the truth of it when I come to narrate the events of my own life: some stories are charming in themselves, while in the case of others everything depends on the way in which they are told. By this I mean to say that there are some that give us pleasure when told without preamble or verbal ornaments of any sort; and there are others that have to be decked out in words and set off with facial expressions, gestures, and inflections of the voice, in such a way that something is made out of trifles and pale and flabby narratives take on point and give pleasure.

What, then, is a novel?

3

The Epic

ONE thing at any rate is very clear: what the reader of the past century was looking for under the title of "novel" has nothing to do with what ancient times sought in the epic. To derive the former from the latter is to close the way to our understanding of the changes in the novelistic genre, if by such changes we understand chiefly the literary evolution which came to maturity in the novel of the nineteenth century.

The novel and the epic are precisely poles apart. The theme of the epic is the past as such: it speaks to us about a world which was and which is no longer, of a mythical age whose antiquity is not a past in the same sense as any remote historical time. It is true that local piety kept gradually linking Homeric men and gods to the citizens of the present by means of slender threads, but this net of geneological traditions does not succeed in bridging the absolute gap which exists between the mythical *yesterday* and the real *today*. No matter how many real yesterdays we interpolate, the sphere inhabited by the Achilleses and the Agamemnons has no relationship with our existence and we cannot reach it, step by step, by retracing the path opened up by the march of time. The epic past is not *our* past. Our past is thinkable as having been the present once, but the epic past eludes identification with any possible present, and when we try to get back to it by means of recollection it gallops away from us like Diomedes' horses, forever at the same distance ahead of us. No, it is not a remembered past, but an ideal past.

If the poet asks *Mneme*, Memory, to tell him about the Achaean sufferings, he does not have recourse to his own subjective memory but to a cosmic memory which he supposes to be latent in the universe. *Mneme* is not the reminiscence of an individual but an elemental power.

This essential remoteness of the legendary protects epic objects from corruption. The same reason that prevents us from bringing them too close to us and from giving them too much youth—the youth of present-day things—preserves their bodies from the effects of old age. The eternal freshness and everlasting mild fragrance of the Homeric poetry are attributable to the inability to become old rather than to a tenacious youthfulness, because old age would not be old if the aging process were to stop. Things become old because each hour as it passes takes them farther from us *ad infinitum*. The old grows older all the time. Achilles, on the other hand, is not any further from us than from Plato.

4

Poetry of the Past

It is time to abandon the opinions held on Homer by the philology of a hundred years ago. Homer is not ingenuousness nor is he a temperament of the dawn of history. Today everyone knows that the *Iliad*, at least our *Iliad*, has never been understood by ordinary people. That is, it was an archaic work from the beginning. The bard was composing in a conventional language which sounded even to him like something old, sacramental and crude. The customs which he assigned to the characters were also of primeval harshness.

Who would have believed it? Homer, an archaic author; the infancy of poetry just an archaeological fiction! Who would have believed it? It is not merely a question of there being archaism in the epic but that the epic *is* an archaism and nothing else essentially. The theme of the epic is the ideal past, the absolute antiquity, we have said. Now we add that archaism is the literary form of the epic, the instrument of poetry-making.

This seems to me to be of the utmost importance if we are to see clearly the meaning of the novel. After Homer, Greece required many centuries to accept the present as a poetic possibility. Actually she never accepted it wholeheartedly. Only what was ancient was poetic for Greece, or rather what was primary in order of time. It is not what Romanticism called ancient, which resembles too closely the antiques of second-hand dealers, with their morbid appeal and our perverse delight in their ruinlike, worm-eaten, fermented and decrepit qualities. All these dying things have only a reflected beauty, and it is not they but the wave of emotion they arouse in us that is the source of poetry; while for the Greek, beauty was an intimate attribute of essential things. What was accidental and momentary seemed to him to be devoid of it. They had a rationalistic sense of esthetics * which prevented them from separating poetic from metaphysical values. They considered beautiful that which contained in itself the origin and the norm, the cause and the model of phenomena. This closed universe of the epic myth is made up exclusively of essential and exemplary objects which were reality when this world of ours had not yet begun to exist.

Between the epic world and the one which surrounds us there was no communication, either great or small. All this life of ours with its today and its yesterday belongs to a second stage of cosmic life. We are part of a second-rate and decayed reality: the men who surround us are not men in the same sense as Ulysses and Hector, so much so that we are not sure whether Ulysses and Hector are men or gods. The gods were then more on the level of men because the latter were divine. Where does the god end and the man begin for Homer? The problem reveals the decadence of our world. The epic figures correspond to an extinct fauna, the character of which is precisely the lack of distinction between god and man, or at least the contiguity of both species. The transition between the two requires no more steps than the frailty of a goddess or the lust of a god.

In short, for the Greeks, only the earliest things are fully poetic, not because they are old but because they are the oldest, because they contain in themselves the

* The concept of proportion, of measure, which always came to Greek lips when speaking of art, shows clearly its mathematical musculature.

foundations and the causes.* The stock of myths which made up at the same time the traditional religion, physics, and history contains all the poetic material of Greek art in its best period. The poet has to start from it, and move within it, although it may be to alter it, as the tragic poets do. These men cannot conceive that a poetic object could be invented, just as we could not conceive inventing a mechanical law. This marks the limitation of Greek epic and of Greek art in general, since until its time of decadence the latter never succeeds in breaking away from its mythical uterus.

Homer believes that the events happened as his hexameters tell us; his audience believed it too. Moreover, Homer does not claim to tell anything new. What he tells, his audience already knows, and Homer knows that they know it. His work is not really creative and he avoids surprising his listener. It is simply an artistic rather than a poetic labor, a technical virtuosity. The only other work in the history of art in which I find an artistic intention comparable to that of the Greek bard is in the resplendent doors of the Florentine Baptistry. Ghiberti, who carved them, was not very much interested in the objects represented but was driven by a wild delight to represent, to transcribe into bronze, figures of men, animals, trees, rocks, fruit.

So it is with Homer. The gentle flow of the epic stream, the rhythmical calm with which equal attention is paid to the great and to the small, would be absurd if we imagine the poet preoccupied with the invention of his plot. The poetic theme existed beforehand once and for all: it sufficed to make it an actual experience in the hearts of the listeners, to make it fully present. That is why it is

* "It was believed that the most sacred is the immemorial, the most ancient" says Aristotle, referring to mythical thought. *Metaphysics*, 893, b, 33.

not absurd to devote only four lines to the death of a hero
and all of two to the closing of a door. Telemachus' nurse

left the apartment; pulling on the silver ring
she closed the door after her, and made fast the bolt in the slot.

5

The Bard

THE esthetic commonplaces of our time may cause us to misinterpret the satisfaction which the sweet blind singer of Ionia felt in making the beautiful things of the past visible. It may actually occur to us to call it realism. Terrible, uncomfortable word! What would a Greek do with it if we were to slip it into his consciousness? For us the real is the perceptible, what our eyes and ears pour into us. We have been brought up by a spiteful age which has beaten the universe into a sheet and made of it a surface, a mere appearance. When we look for reality we search for appearances. But the Greek took reality to be the opposite: the real is the essential, the profound and latent; not the external appearance but the living sources of all appearance. Plotinus could never make up his mind to have his portrait made because this was, according to him, to bequeath to the world the shadow of a shadow.

The epic poet, with the baton in his hand, rises in our midst, turning his blind face vaguely towards the brightest light; the sun is for him a father's hand which, in the night, touches a son's cheeks; his body has learned the motion of the heliotrope and tries to receive the broad caress as it passes. His lips quiver a little like the strings of an instrument being tuned up. What is his desire? He would like to put the things that happened clearly before us. He begins to speak. But no, this is not speaking, it is reciting. The words come in a disciplined way and they seem to be disassociated from the trivial existence which they had in ordinary speech. Like an ascending apparatus, the hexameter holds the words suspended in an imaginary air and keeps their feet off the ground. This is symbolic. This is what the bard wants: to remove us from everyday reality. The phrases are ritualistic, the expressions solemn and slightly hieratic, the syntax archaic. From the present he takes only the flower. An occasional comparison drawn from the unchanging, basic phenomena of the cosmos—the sea, the wind, the wild beasts, the birds—injects into the ancient trunk the sap of actuality strictly necessary for the past, as such, to take possession of us and dislodge the present.

Such is the practice of the bard, such is his role in the construction of an epic work. Unlike the modern poet he is not afflicted by the hankering after originality. He knows that his song is not his alone. The racial spirit, creator of the myth, had accomplished the main task before he was born; it had created the beautiful objects. The poet's role is reduced to the scrupulousness of a craftsman.

6

Helen and Madame Bovary

I do not understand how a Spaniard, a teacher of Greek, could say that it facilitates the comprehension of the *Iliad* to imagine a struggle between the youths from two Castilian towns for the possession of a handsome village girl. I can understand being told about Madame Bovary that we should turn our attention towards the typical woman of the provinces practicing adultery. This would be fitting: the novelist completes his task when he has succeeded in representing for us in concrete form what we already knew in the abstract.* As we close the book we say: "Adulterous women in the provinces are actually like this; and these rural assemblies are really rural assemblies." We have satisfied the novelist with that reaction. But reading the *Iliad* it does not occur to us to congratulate Homer, because his Achilles is certainly a good Achilles, a perfect Achilles, and his Helen an unmistakable Helen. The epic figures are not representatives of types but unique creatures. Only one Achilles has existed and only one Helen; only one war on the bank of the Scamander. If we were to think of the careless wife of Menelaus as just an ordinary woman, courted by an enemy of her country, Homer would have failed. Because his mission was very restricted, not free like that of Ghiberti or Flaubert, he has to make us see this Helen and this Achilles, who, luckily, do not resemble the humans we

* "Ma pauvre Bovary sans doute souffre et pleure dans vingt villages de France à la fois, à cette heure même." Flaubert: *Correspondance*, II, 284.

126

usually meet at the crossroads.

The epic is at first the creation of unique beings, of "heroic" natures: the age-old popular fantasy performs this first operation. Later on, the epic becomes the realization, the full evocation of those beings, and this is the task of the bard.

In this roundabout way we have gained, I believe, some light which makes the meaning of the novel clear to us, for what we find in the novel is the opposite of the epic genre. If the theme of the latter is the past, as such, that of the novel is the present as such. If the epic figures are invented, if they are unique and incomparable natures, which in themselves have poetic value, the characters of the novel are typical and nonpoetic; they are taken, not from the myth, which is already an esthetic and creative element or atmosphere, but from the street, from the physical world, from the living environment of the author and the reader. We have cleared up a third point: literary art is not the whole of poetry, but only a secondary poetic activity. Art is the technique, it is the mechanism of realization before which the actual creation or invention of beautiful objects appears as the primary and supreme poetic function. That mechanism may be and must be realistic on certain occasions, but not necessarily and not in all cases. The desire for realism, characteristic of our times, cannot be raised to the rank of a norm. We like the illusion of apparent reality, but other ages have had other preferences. It would be vanity to presume that the human race has always wanted and will always want the same things as we do. No, let us open our hearts wide so that they may catch in them all the human things which are alien to us. Let us prefer to have unruly diversity rather than monotonous conformity on earth.

7

The Myth, Leaven of History

THE epic perspective which consists, as we have seen, in looking at the events of the world from certain cardinal myths (the summits as it were) does not die with Greece. It has come down to us. It will never die. It is true that when people ceased to believe in the cosmogonic and historical reality of their narratives, the good days of the Hellenic race came to an end. But even deprived of all religious significance, the epic themes, the mythical seeds not only endure as splendid irreplaceable phantoms, but they gain in liveliness and plastic force. Hoarded in literary memory, or hidden in the subsoil of the collective memory, they constitute a poetic leaven of incalculable energy. Bring the true history of a king, an Antiochus or an Alexander, for example, close to this incandescent material and the real history will begin to burn on all sides: all that was normal and ordinary in it will be utterly reduced to ashes. Then, after the fire there will remain before our astonished eyes, shining like a diamond, the marvelous history of a magical Apollonius,* or of a miraculous Alexander. This marvelous history, is, of course, not history: it has been called a novel. In this way it has been possible to speak of the Greek novel, but the ambiguity which exists in this word becomes evident now. The Greek novel is only corrupted history, divinely corrupted by the myth, or rather, like the voyage to the country of the Arimaspi, fantastic geography, memories

* The figure of Apollonius is based on material from the story of Antiochus.

128

of voyages which the myth has distorted and later put together again freely. To the same genre belongs all literature of the imagination, all that is called story, ballad, legend, and books of chivalry. They always deal with some historical material which the myth has distorted and reabsorbed.

We should not forget that the myth is the representative of a world different from ours. If ours is the real one, the mythical world will appear unreal to us. At any rate, what is possible in one is impossible in the other; the mechanics of our planetary system do not apply in the mythical system. The reabsorption of a terrestrial event by a myth consists, then, in turning it into a physical and historical impossibility. The earthly material remains, but it is subject to laws so different from those existing in our world that it is tantamount to having no laws as far as we are concerned.

The epic will exert its beneficent influence over humanity to the end of time through its child, the literature of the imagination, which will duplicate the universe, bringing us frequent news of a delightful world where, if the gods of Homer no longer dwell, their legitimate successors rule. The gods stand for a dynasty under which the impossible is possible. The normal does not exist where they reign; all-embracing disorder emanates from their thrones. The constitution they have sworn to obey has one single article: adventure is permitted.

8

Books of Chivalry

WHEN the vision of the world which the myth supplies
is deprived of its command over human souls by its hostile sister, science, the epic loses its religious gravity and
dashes forth in search of adventures. The *libros de caba-
llerías*, or books of chivalrous adventures, were the last
great sprouting from the old epic trunk—at least, the last
so far.

The book of chivalry retains the epic characteristics,
except the belief in the reality of what is told.* The
events related in it are considered as old too, with an ideal
antiquity. The good old days of King Arthur are like
backdrops of a conventional past which hang vaguely,
indistinctly over the chronology. Apart from the repartee
of some dialogues, the poetic instrument in the book of
chivalry is, as in the epic, the narrative. I disagree with
the accepted opinion which makes narrative the instrument of the novel. This opinion is the consequence of not
having contrasted the two genres confused under the
name of novel. The book of imagination narrates, but the
novel describes. The narrative is the form in which the
past exists for us, and it is possible to narrate only what
has happened, that is to say, what no longer exists. One
describes, on the other hand, what is present. The epic
had, as is known, an ideal preterite—the narrative past—

---

* I would say that, in a certain way, even this is retained. But I
would be forced to write many pages, unnecessary here, about
that mysterious kind of hallucination which lies, undoubtedly, in
the pleasure felt when we read a book of chivalry.

which is known in grammars as the epic or gnomic aorist.

On the other hand, description interests us in the novel precisely because we are not actually interested in what is described. We disregard the objects which are placed before us in order to pay attention to the manner in which they are presented. Neither Sancho, nor the priest, nor the barber, nor the Knight of the Green Overcoat, nor Madame Bovary, nor her husband, nor the foolish Homais are interesting. We would not give two cents to see them. But we would give away a kingdom for the satisfaction of seeing them captured within the confines of the two famous books. I do not understand how this has passed unnoticed by those who think about esthetic questions. What we pitilessly tend to call boring is a whole literary genre, although one that has failed. The boredom consists in the narration of something which does not interest us.* The narrative must be justified by its subject matter, and the more superficial it is, the less it comes between the events and ourselves, the better it will be.

The author of the book of chivalry, then, in contrast to the novelist, directs all his poetic energy towards the invention of interesting events. These are the adventures. Today we could read the *Odyssey* as a tale of adventure; the work would doubtless lose nobility and significance, but we would not have misjudged entirely its esthetic intention. Below Ulysses, the equal of the gods, peeps Sinbad the Sailor and, much more remotely, the homely bourgeois muse of Jules Verne. The connection is based on the fact that events are directed by whim. In the *Odyssey* whim is hallowed by the different humors of the gods; in the books of fiction, of chivalry, it shows its nature more cynically. If in the old poem the wander-

---

* In a number of *La Critica* Croce mentions the definition which an Italian gives of a *bore:* one who takes away our solitude and does not give us companionship.

ings gain heightened interest because they come from the whim of a god—a theological reason after all—the adventure is interesting in itself because of its inherent capriciousness.

If we examine more closely our ordinary notion of reality,[19] perhaps we should find that we do not consider real what actually happens but a certain manner of happening that is familiar to us. In this vague sense, then, the real is not so much what is seen as foreseen; not so much what we see as what we know. When a series of events takes an unforeseen turn, we say that it seems incredible. That is why our ancestors called the adventure story a fiction. Adventure shatters the oppressive, insistent reality as if it were a piece of glass. It is the unforeseen, the unthought-of, the new. Each adventure is a new birth of the world, a unique process. How can it fail to be interesting?

Soon after we begin living we become aware of the confines of our prison. It takes us thirty years at the most to recognize the limits within which our possibilities will move. We take stock of reality, which is like measuring the length of the chain which binds our feet. Then we say: "Is this life? Nothing more than this? A closed cycle which is repeated, always identical?" This is a dangerous hour for every man.

In this connection I recall an admirable drawing of Gavarni. It is of a sly old man near a stage where the world is shown through a peep-hole. The old man is saying: "Il faut montrer à l'homme des images, la réalité l'embête!" Gavarni was living among some Parisian writers and artists who were defenders of esthetic realism. The ease with which the public was attracted by the tales of adventure made him indignant. The fact is that weak races may turn this strong drug of the imagination into a vice, an easy escape from the heavy weight of existence.

9

Master Pedro's Puppet Show

As the thread of the adventure develops we experience an increasing emotional tension, as if by accompanying the former in its course we felt ourselves violently pulled away from the line followed by inert reality. At each step this reality pulls, threatening to make the event conform with the natural course of events, and it is necessary for a new impulse from the adventurous power to free it and push it towards greater impossibilities. We are carried along in the adventure as if within a missile, and in the dynamic struggle between it, as it advances on an escaping tangent, and the center of the earth which tries to restrain it, we side with the missile. This partiality of ours increases with each incident and adds to a kind of hallucination, in which we take the adventure for an instant as actual reality.

Cervantes has represented in a marvelous way this psychological reaction of the reader of fables in the experience undergone by the spirit of Don Quixote in the presence of Master Pedro's puppet show. The horse of Don Gaiferos in his headlong gallop leaves a vacuum behind him, into which a current of hallucinating air rushes, sweeping along with it everything that is not firmly fixed on the ground. There the soul of Don Quixote, light as thistledown, snatched up in the illusory vortex, goes whirling like a dry leaf; and in its pursuit everything ingenuous and sorrowing still left in the world will go forevermore.

The frame of the puppet show which Master Pedro

goes around presenting is the dividing line between two
continents of the mind. Within, the puppet show encloses a fantastic world, articulated by the genius of the
impossible. It is the world of adventure, of imagination,
of myth. Without there is a room in which several un-
sophisticated men are gathered, men like those we see
every day, concerned with the daily struggle to live. In
their midst is a fool, a knight from the neighborhood,
who, one morning, abandoned his town impelled by a
small anatomical anomaly of the brain. Nothing prevents
us from entering this room: we could breathe in its atmosphere and touch those present on the shoulder, since
they are made of the same stuff and condition as ourselves. However, this room is, in its turn, included in a
book, that is to say, in another puppet show larger than
the first. If we should enter the room, we would have
stepped inside an ideal object, we would be moving in
the hollow interior of an esthetic body. (Velázquez in
The Maids of Honor offers us an analogous case: he is
painting a picture of the king and queen and at the same
time he has placed his studio in the picture. In *The Spin-
ners* he has united forever the legendary action represented by a tapestry to the humble room in which it was
manufactured.) Along a conduit of simple-mindedness
and dementia emanations come and go from one continent
to the other, from the puppet show to the room, from
the room to the puppet show. One would say that the important thing is precisely the osmosis and endosmosis between the two.

10

Poetry and Reality

CERVANTES declares that he is writing his book against the books of chivalry. Recent criticism has tended to lose sight of this purpose of Cervantes. Perhaps it has been thought that it was a manner of speaking, a conventional presentation of the work, as was the exemplary tinge with which he covers his short novels. Nevertheless, one must return to this point of view. For esthetic purposes it is essential to see the work of Cervantes as a polemic against books of chivalry. Otherwise, how can one understand the incalculable broadening it brings to literary art? The epic plane on which imaginary objects glide was until now the only one, and poetry could be defined in the same terms as the epic.* But now the imaginary plane comes to be a second plane. Art is enriched by one more aspect; it is, so to speak, enlarged by a third dimension; it reaches an esthetic depth, which like geometric depth, presuppposes a plurality of aspects. Consequently, the poetic can no longer be made to consist of that special attraction of the ideal past or of the interest which its procedure, always new, unique, and surprising, lends to adventure. Now our poetry has to be capable of coping with present reality.

Note the stringency of the problem. So far we had arrived at the poetic by transcending and abandoning the circumstantial, the actual; so that to speak of "actual reality" was equivalent to saying "non-poetic." We have

* We have ignored lyric poetry from the outset, since it is an independent esthetic tendency.

here then the greatest conceivable esthetic extension of the poetic. How could the inn and Sancho and the muleteer and the blustering Master Pedro be poetic? Of course they are not poetic. In contrast with the puppet show they stand formally for the attack on the poetic. Cervantes sets Sancho against every adventure in order to make it impossible when it happens to Sancho. This is Sancho's mission. We do not see, then, how the field of poetry can be spread over the real. While the imaginary was poetic in itself, reality is anti-poetic *per se*. *Hic Rhodus, hic salta:* here is where esthetics must sharpen its vision. Contrary to what the naivete of our learned researchers supposes, it is the realistic tendency that is in greater need of justification and explanation; it is the *exemplum crucis* of esthetics. Actually, it might be unintelligible if the great gestures of Don Quixote did not succeed in guiding us. On which side of the show shall we place Don Quixote? It would be wrong to choose either continent. Don Quixote stands at the intersection where both worlds meet forming a beveled edge.[20] If we are told that Don Quixote belongs entirely to reality we shall not object. We would only remark that with Don Quixote his untamed will would become part of that reality. This will is obsessed with one single goal: adventure. Don Quixote, who is real, actually wants to have adventures. As he himself says: "The sorcerers may take away my good fortune, but not my courage and spirit." Hence the astonishing ease with which he passes from the audience to the puppet show. His is a frontier nature, as the nature of man generally is, according to Plato.

Perhaps we did not suspect a moment ago what is happening now: that reality is coming into poetry to raise adventure to a higher esthetic power. If this were confirmed we should see reality opening up to make room for the imaginary continent and serve as its support, in the same way as the inn on a moonlit night becomes a ship which sails over the parched Manchegan plains carrying within it Charlemagne and the Twelve Peers, Marsiles of Sansueña and the peerless Mélisande. The fact is that what is related in the books of chivalry has reality in the imagination of Don Quixote, who, in his turn, enjoys an unquestionable existence. So that, although the realistic novel was born in opposition to the so-called novel of fantasy, it carries adventure enclosed within its body.

11

Reality, Leaven of the Myth

THE new poetry which Cervantes practices cannot have as simple a contexture as the Greek and the medieval. Cervantes looks at the world from the height of the Renaissance. The Renaissance has tightened things a little more and has completely overcome the old sensibility. With his physics, Galileo lays down the stern laws which govern the universe. A new system has begun; everything is confined within stricter forms. Adventures are impossible in this new order of things. Before long, Leibnitz would declare that simple possibility lacks any validity; that only the "*compossible*" is possible, that is to say, what is closely connected with the natural laws.* In this way the possible, which shows its crusty independence in the myth, in the miracle, is inserted into the real as the adventure in Cervantes' portrayal of truth.

Another characteristic of the Renaissance is the predominance acquired by the psychological. The ancient world seems a mere body without any inner recesses and secrets. The Renaissance discovers the inner world in all its vast extension, the *me ipsum*, the consciousness, the subjective. *Quixote* is the flower of this great new turn which culture takes. In it the epic comes to an end forever, along with its aspiration to support a mythical world bordering on that of material phenomena but

* For Aristotle and the Middle Ages anything that does not contain contradiction in itself is possible. What is "*compossible*" needs more. For Aristotle the centaur is possible; for us it is not, because biology, natural science, does not tolerate it.

different from it. It is true that the reality of the adventure is saved, but such a salvation involves the sharpest irony. The reality of the adventure is reduced to the psychological, perhaps to a biological humor. It is real insofar as it is vapor from a brain, so that its reality is rather that of its opposite, the material.

In summer the sun pours down torrents of fire on La Mancha, and frequently the burning earth produces the effect of a mirage. The water which we see is not real water, but there is something real in it: its source. This bitter source, which produces the water of the mirage, is the desperate dryness of the land. We can experience a similar phenomenon in two directions: one simple and straight, seeing the water which the sun depicts as actual; another ironic, oblique, seeing it as a mirage, that is to say, seeing through the coolness of the water the dryness of the earth in disguise. The ingenuous manner of experiencing imaginary and significant things is found in the novel of adventure, the tale, the epic; the oblique manner in the realistic novel. The latter needs the mirage to make us see it as such. So it is not only that *Quixote* was written against the books of chivalry, and as a result bears them within it, but that the novel as a literary genre consists essentially of such an absorption.

This provides an explanation of what seemed inexplicable: how reality, the actual, can be changed into poetic substance. By itself, seen in a direct way, it would never be poetic: this is the privilege of the mythical. But we can consider it obliquely as destruction of the myth, as criticism of the myth. In this form reality, which is of an inert and meaningless nature, quiet and mute, acquires movement, is changed into an active power of aggression against the crystal orb of the ideal. The enchantment of the latter broken, it falls into fine, iridescent dust which gradually loses its colors until it becomes an earthy brown.

We witness this scene in every novel. So, strictly speaking, it is not reality that becomes poetic or enters into the work of art but only that gesture or movement of reality in which the ideal is reabsorbed.

In conclusion, the process we have here is exactly the opposite of the one engendered by the novel of fantasy. Furthermore, the realistic novel describes the process itself, while the novel of fantasy describes only the product, the adventure.

12

The Windmills

THE plain of Montiel is now for us a reverberant, limitless area where all kinds of things may be found illustrated. Riding over it with Don Quixote and Sancho, we come to understand that things have two sides. One is the "sense" of things, their meaning, what they are when interpreted. The other is the "materiality" of things, the positive substance that constitutes them before, and independent of, any interpretation.[21]

The flour mills of Criptana rise and gesticulate above the horizon in the bloodshot sunset. These mills have a meaning: their "sense" as giants.[22] It is true that Don Quixote is out of his senses but the problem is not solved by declaring Don Quixote insane. What is abnormal in him has been and will continue to be normal in humanity. Granted that these giants are not giants, but what about the others? I mean, what about giants in general? Where did man get his giants? Because they never existed nor do they exist in reality. Whenever it may have been, the occasion on which man first thought up giants does not differ essentially from the scene in Cervantes' work. There would always be something which was not a giant, but which tended to become one if regarded from its idealistic side. Thus there is an allusion to Briarean arms in the turning wings of these windmills. If we obey the impulse of that allusion and let ourselves go along the curve indicated by it, we shall arrive at a giant.

Justice and truth, too, like all expressions of the spirit, are mirages produced on matter. Culture—the ideal side of things—tries to set itself up as a separate and self-sufficient world to which we can transfer our hearts. This is an illusion, and only looked upon as an illusion, only considered as a mirage on earth, does culture take its proper place.[23]

13

Realistic Poetry

IN the same way as the outlines of rocks and clouds contain allusions to certain animal forms, all things from their inert materiality make signs, as it were, which we interpret. These interpretations coalesce into an objectivity which is like a duplication of the primary, or so-called real, objectivity.[24] An everlasting conflict originates from this: the "idea" or "sense" of each thing and its "materiality" trying to fit into each other. But this implies the victory of one of them. If the "idea" triumphs, the "materiality" is superseded and we live under a hallucination. If the materiality wins out and, penetrating the vapors of the idea, reabsorbs it, we live disillusioned.

It is known that the action of seeing consists in applying a previous image which we have to a present sensation. A dark point in the distance may be seen by us successively as a tower, as a tree, as a man. We find that Plato was right when he explained perception as the result of something which goes from the eye to the object and something which comes from the object to the eye. Leonardo da Vinci used to place his students in front of a wall so that they might get accustomed to noticing a great number of imaginary forms in the shapes of the stones, in their joining lines, in the play of light and shade. Platonic to the core, all that Leonardo was looking for in reality was the Paraclete, the awakener of the spirit.

Now there are distances, lights, and slants from which the sensitive material of things reduces the sphere of our interpretation to a minimum. The force of the concrete in things stops the movement of our images. The inert and harsh object rejects whatever "meanings" we may give it; it is just there, confronting us, affirming its mute, terrible materiality in the face of all phantoms. This is what we call realism: to put things at a certain distance, place them under a light, slant them in such a way that the stress falls upon the side which slopes down toward pure materiality.[25]

The myth is always the starting point of all poetry, including the realistic, except that in the latter we accompany the myth in its descent, in its fall. This collapse of the poetic is the theme of realistic poetry. I do not believe that reality can enter into art in any way other than by making an active and combative element out of its own inertia and desolation. It cannot interest us by itself. Much less can its duplication interest us. As I said above, the characters of the novel lack attraction. How then can their representation move us? And yet, it is so: the real things do not move us but their representation—that is to say, the representation of their reality—does. This distinction is, in my opinion, decisive: the poetic quality of reality does not lie in the reality of this or that particular thing, but in reality as a generic function.[26] Therefore it does not actually matter what objects the realist chooses to describe. Any one at all will do, since they all have an imaginary halo around them, and the point is to show the pure materiality under it. We see in this materiality its final claim, its critical power before which, providing it is declared sufficient, man's pretension to the ideal, to all that he loves and imagines, yields; the insufficiency, in a word, of culture, of all that is noble, clear, lofty—this is the significance of poetic realism. Cervantes recognizes that culture is all that, but that, alas, it is a fiction. Surrounding culture—as the puppet-show of fancy was surrounded by the inn—lies the barbarous, brutal, mute, meaningless reality of things. It is sad that it should reveal itself to us thus, but what can we do about it! It is real, it is there: it is terribly self-sufficient. Its force and its single meaning are rooted in its sheer presence. Culture is memories and promises, an irreversible past, a dreamed future. But reality is a simple and frightening "being there." It is a presence, a deposit, an inertia. It is materiality* [27]

* The intention of realism becomes still more obvious in painting. Raphael and Michelangelo paint the forms of things. The form is always ideal—an image of memory or a construction of ours. Velázquez seeks the impression of things. The impression is formless and stresses the material—satin, velvet, linen, wood, organic protoplasm—of which things are made.

14

Mime

CERVANTES does not, of course, invent *a nihilo* the poetic theme of reality: he simply carries it to a classical expansion. Until it finds in the novel, in *Quixote*, the organic structure which suits it, that theme has been wandering like a trickle of water seeking its outlet, haltingly feeling its way among obstacles, searching for a way around them, infiltrating other bodies. At any rate it has strange beginnings. It originates in the antipodes of the myth and the epic. Strictly speaking, it originates outside of literature.

The germ of realism is found in a certain impulse which forces man to imitate the outstanding characteristic of his fellows or of animals. That characteristic feature of a physiognomy—person, animal, or thing—is so significant that, on being reproduced, it evokes in us the other characteristics, making them present to us quickly and vividly. However, one does not imitate for the sake of imitating: this imitative impulse—like the most complex forms of realism which have been described above—is not original, it is not self-created. It grows out of an extraneous aim. One imitates in order to mock. Here we have the origin for which we are searching: the mime. So that it is only through a comic intention that reality seems to acquire an esthetic interest. This seems to be a very curious historical confirmation of what I have just said about the novel.

Actually, in Greece, where poetry demands an ideal distance from every object in order to make it esthetic, we find everyday themes only in comedy. Like Cervantes, Aristophanes makes use of the people he meets in the market place and introduces them into an artistic work, but he does it in order to make fun of them. From comedy, dialogue originates in its turn—a genre which has not been able to achieve independence. Plato's dialogue also both describes the real and makes fun of the real. Whenever it goes beyond the comic it leans upon an extra-poetic interest—the scientific. This is a fact to keep in mind. The real, either as comedy or as science, may pass into poetry, but we never find the poetry of the real as simply real.

Here we have the only points of Greek literature to which we can fasten the thread of novelistic evolution.* The novel is born with a comic sting and it will preserve this nature forever. The criticism, the banter, is not an unessential ornament of *Quixote*, but rather the very texture of the genre, perhaps of all realism.

* The love story—the *Erotici*—derives from the new comedy. See Wilamowitz-Moellendorf in *Greek Historical Writing*, 1908, pp. 22–23.

15

The Hero [28]

So far we have not had the opportunity of looking carefully at the essence of the comic. When I was writing
that the novel shows us a mirage as such, the word
comedy kept circling around the tip of my pen like a
dog who hears his master's call. For some unknown
reason a certain similarity makes us compare the mirage
on the burnt-stubble fields with the comedies in the
minds of men.

Now our story leads us back to this subject. We had
left something hanging in mid-air, wavering between the
room in the inn and Master Pedro's puppet show. This
something is nothing less than the will of Don Quixote.
People may be able to take good fortune away from this
neighbor of ours, but they will not be able to take away
his effort and courage. His adventures may be the vapors
of a fermenting brain, but his will for adventure is real
and true. Now, adventure is a dislocation of the material
order, something unreal. In this will for adventure, in
this effort and courage, we come across a strange dual
nature, whose two elements belong to opposite worlds:
the will is real but what is willed is not real.[29]

Such a phenomenon is unknown in the epic. The men
of Homer belong to the same world as their desires. In
Don Quixote we have, on the other hand, a man who
wishes to reform reality. But is he not a piece of that
reality? Does he not live off it, is he not a consequence
of it? How is it possible for that which does not exist—
a projected adventure—to govern and alter harsh real-

148

ity? [30] Perhaps it is not possible, but it is a fact that there are men who decide not to be satisfied with reality. Such men aim at altering the course of things; they refuse to repeat the gestures that custom, tradition, or biological instincts force them to make. These men we call heroes, because to be a hero means to be one out of many, to be oneself.[31] If we refuse to have our actions determined by heredity or environment it is because we seek to base the origin of our actions on ourselves and only on ourselves. The hero's will is not that of his ancestors nor of his society, but his own. This will to be oneself is heroism.

I do not think that there is any more profound originality than this "practical," active originality of the hero.[32] His life is a perpetual resistance to what is habitual and customary. Each movement that he makes has first had to overcome custom and invent a new kind of gesture. Such a life is a perpetual suffering, a constant tearing oneself away from that part of oneself which is given over to habit and is a prisoner of matter.

16

Intervention of Lyricism

FACED with the fact of heroic action—the will to adventure—we can adopt two attitudes: either we rush with it toward sorrow, because we consider that the heroic life has "meaning," or we give reality the slight push which is enough to destroy all heroism, as a dream is shattered by shaking the sleeper. Previously I have called these two directions of our interest the straight and the oblique. It should be emphasized now that the core of reality, to which both refer, is one and the same. The difference, then, comes from the subjective way in which we approach it. So, if the epic and the novel differ in the objectives—the past and reality—there is still room for a new division within the theme of reality. But this division is no longer based on the object alone; it springs from a subjective element, from our attitude towards that theme.

In the foregoing, lyricism, which is the other source of poetry as opposed to the epic, has been completely left out. This is not the place to seek its essence nor to stop to meditate on what lyricism may be. The time for that will come later. Let it be sufficient to remember what is admitted by everyone: lyricism is an esthetic projection of the general tonality of our feelings. The epic is neither sad nor gay: it is an Olympian, indifferent art full of forms of eternal, ageless objects; it is an extrinsic, invulnerable art.

A changeable and wavering substance enters art with lyricism. The sensibility of man varies in the course of the centuries, with its polarity gravitating sometimes eastwards, sometimes westwards. There are gay times and times of bitterness. It all depends on whether the estimate which man makes of his own worth seems to him favorable or unfavorable in the last resort.

I do not believe that it was necessary to insist upon what was suggested at the beginning of this short treatise: that poetry and all art deals with the human and only the human—whether the theme of poetry be the past or the present. A landscape is always painted as a background for man. This being so, it cannot help but follow that all forms of art find their origin in the changing interpretations of man by man. Tell me what you feel about man and I shall tell you which art you cultivate.

Since every literary genre, even allowing for some marginal overflow, is a river bed which one of these interpretations of man has opened up, nothing is less surprising than the preference of each epoch for a particular genre. That is why the authentic literature of a period is a general confession of the human spirit at that time.

Returning now to the fact of heroism, we note that sometimes it has been looked at directly and other times obliquely. In the first instance, our glance changed the hero into an esthetic object which we call tragedy. In the second, it made of him an esthetic object which we call comedy. There have been periods which have had scarcely any feeling for the tragic, times saturated with humor and comedy. The nineteenth century—a bourgeois, democratic and positivist century—has been excessively inclined to see comedy on earth. The correlation which we have drawn between the epic and the novel is repeated here between the tragic and the comic tendency of our spirit.

17

Tragedy

A HERO, I have said, is one who wants to be himself.[33] The root of heroic action may be found, then, in a real act of the will. There is nothing like that in the epic. For this reason Don Quixote is not an epic figure, but he is a hero. Achilles makes the epic, the hero wants it. So that the tragic character is not tragic, and therefore, poetic, in so far as he is a man of flesh and blood, but only in so far as he wills. The will—that paradoxical object which begins in reality and ends in the ideal, since one only wants what is not—is the tragic theme; and an epoch for which the will does not exist, a deterministic and Darwinian epoch, for example, cannot be interested in tragedy.

Let us not fix our attention too much on the Greek tragedy. If we are sincere, we shall admit that we do not understand it very well. Even philology has not equipped our understanding sufficiently to follow a Greek tragedy. Perhaps there is no work more interspersed with purely historical, transitory motives. We should not forget that it was a religious function in Athens, so that the play takes place within the hearts of the spectators even more than on the boards of the theater. An extra-poetic atmosphere—religion—surrounds the stage and the audience. What has come down to us is like the libretto of an opera, the music of which we have never heard; or like the wrong side of a tapestry woven by faith, showing only the multicolored threads. The Hellenists are puzzled by the Athenians' faith, which they do not know how to reconstruct. Until they find out, Greek tragedy will be a page written in a language for which we do not have a dictionary.

All we see clearly is that the tragic poets of Greece speak to us personally through the masks of their heroes. When does Shakespeare do this? Aeschylus is inspired by a half poetic and half theological motive. His theme is at least as metaphysical and ethical as it is esthetic. I would call him a *theopoet*. The problems of good and evil, of liberty, of justification, of order in the cosmos, of universal causes trouble him. His works are a progressive series of attacks upon these divine questions. His inspiration seems rather like an impulse of religious reform. He resembles a Saint Paul or a Luther more than an "homme de lettres." By dint of piety he would like to go beyond a popular religion which is insufficient for the maturity of the times. In another place this impulse would not have led a man towards poetry, but in Greece, since religion was less sacerdotal, more flexible and more environmental, theological interest could be less differentiated from the poetic, the political, and the philosophical.

Let us leave aside, then, Greek drama and all the theories which, basing tragedy on some sort of fate, believe that it is the downfall, the death of the hero which gives it its tragic quality. The intervention of fate is not necessary,[34] and although the hero usually is overcome, the triumph of fate, if it does come, does not take away his heroism. Let us listen to the effect that drama produces on the ordinary spectator. If he is sincere he will have to confess that it really seems a little unlikely to him. Twenty times he has been tempted to get up and advise the protagonist to desist, to abandon his position, because the plain man very sensibly thinks that all the bad things happen to the hero through his persistence in such and such a purpose. By giving it up, he could make everything turn out well and, as the Chinese say at the end of a tale, alluding to their former nomadism, could settle down and raise many children. There is no fate, then, or rather what happens is fated to happen because the hero has caused it. The misfortunes of Calderón's *Constant Prince* were fated from the point when he decided to be constant, but he himself was not made constant by fate.

I believe that the classical theories are the victims here of a simple *quid pro quo,* and that they should be corrected by taking advantage of the impression that heroism produces in the soul of the plain man incapable of heroic acts. The plain man is ignorant of that stream of life in which only sumptuary, superfluous activities take place. He is ignorant of the overflow and excess of vitality. He lives bound to what is necessary and what he does, he does perforce. He is always impelled to act; his actions are reactions. He cannot conceive that anyone should get involved in affairs which are not his concern. Anyone who shows the will for adventure seems a little crazy to him, and in tragedy he sees only a man forced to suffer the consequences of an endeavor which no one forces him to pursue.

Far from the tragic originating in fate, then, it is essential for the hero to want his tragic destiny. Therefore, tragedy always has a fictitious character when regarded from the point of view of the vegetative life. All the sorrow springs from the hero's refusal to give up an ideal part, an imaginary role which he has chosen. The actor in the drama, it might be said paradoxically, plays a part which is, in its turn, the playing of a part, although the latter is played in earnest. At any rate, an entirely free volition originates and produces the tragic process. This "act of will," creating a new series of realities which only exist through it—the tragic order—is naturally a fiction for anyone whose only wishes are those of natural necessity, which is satisfied with what merely exists.

18

Comedy

TRAGEDY is not produced on the ground level. We have to rise to it, be drawn up to it. It is unreal. If we wish to seek something like it in existing things, we must raise our eyes and fix them on the highest peaks of history. Tragedy assumes a predisposition towards great actions in our spirit; otherwise it will appear like bragging. It does not impose itself upon us with the obviousness and forcefulness of realism, which makes the work begin under our very feet and leads us into it without our being aware of it, passively. In a way, for us to enjoy tragedy it is necessary that we too want it a little as the hero wants his destiny. Consequently, it comes to prey upon the symptoms of atrophied heroism which may exist in us, because we all bear within us the rudiments of a hero; but once embarked along the heroic route we shall see that the strong movements and the exalting impetus which inflate tragedy re-echo in our hearts. We shall find with surprise that we are capable of living at a tremendous tension and that everything around us increases its proportions and acquires a superior dignity. Tragedy in the theater opens our eyes so that we can discover and appreciate the heroic in reality. Thus Napoleon, who knew something of psychology, did not wish his traveling company to produce comedies before that audience of conquered sovereigns gathered during his stay in Frankfurt, and he made Talma present the characters of Racine and Corneille.

However, a host of plebeian instincts swarm around the

rudimentary hero that we carry within us. For sufficient reasons, no doubt, we usually cherish a great distrust towards anyone who wants to start new ways. We do not demand justification from those who do not try to step off the beaten track, but we demand it peremptorily from the bold man who does. Our plebeian self hates few things more than it hates an ambitious person, and the hero, of course, begins by being ambitious. Vulgarity does not irritate us as much as pretentiousness. Hence the hero is always only a few inches from falling not into misfortune, for this would be rising to it, but into ridicule. The saying "from the sublime to the ridiculous" formulates this danger which really threatens the hero. Alas for him if he does not justify by an exuberance of greatness, by superlative qualities, his claim not to be like the rest of us, "the run of the mill"! The reformer, the one who attempts a new art, a new science, new politics, spends his lifetime in a hostile, corrosive environment, which supposes him to be a conceited fellow, if not a fraud. He is up against those things the very denial of which makes him a hero: tradition, the accepted, the customary, the ways of our parents, national customs, the typical; in a word, widespread inertia. All this, accumulated in an age-old alluvium, forms a crust several yards deep; and the hero proposes to explode this weighty mass with an idea, which is less than an airy corpuscle suddenly sprung up in his fantasy. The instinct of inertia and self-preservation cannot tolerate it and it avenges itself. It sends realism against him and envelops him in comedy.

Since the character of the heroic lies in the will to be what one is not yet, half of the figure of the tragic protagonist is outside of reality.[35] It is sufficient to pull him by the feet and restore him completely to reality for him to become a comic character. The noble heroic fiction rises above the inertia of reality through the greatest exertions; it lives by aspiration. The future is its witness. The *vis comica* simply accentuates the inclination of the hero towards pure materiality. Reality advances through the fiction, imposes itself on us and reabsorbs the tragic role.* The hero made this role part of himself, he fused himself with it. The reabsorption by reality consists in solidifying, in materializing the aspiring intention of the hero upon his person. In this fashion we see the role as a ridiculous disguise, as a mask beneath which a vulgar creature moves.[36]

The hero anticipates the future and appeals to it. His gestures have a utopian significance. He does not say that he is but that he wants to be. Thus, the feminist woman hopes for the day when women will not need to be feminists. But the comic writer substitutes for the feminists' ideal the modern woman who actually tries to carry out that ideal. As something made to live in a future world, the ideal, when it is drawn back and frozen in the present, does not succeed in satisfying the most trivial functions of existence; and so people laugh. People watch the fall of the ideal bird as it flies over the vapor of stagnant water and they laugh. It is a useful laughter: for each hero whom it hits, it crushes a hundred frauds.

Consequently, comedy lives on tragedy as the novel does on the epic. Comedy was born historically in Greece as a reaction against the tragic poets and the philosophers who wanted to introduce new gods and set up new customs. In the name of popular tradition, of "our forefathers," and of sacred customs, Aristophanes puts on the stage the actual figures of Socrates and Euripides, and

---

* Bergson cites a curious example. The queen of Prussia enters the room where Napoleon is. She is furious, screaming, and threatening. Napoleon confines himself to begging her to sit down. When the queen sits down, she is silent; the tragic role cannot be maintained in the bourgeois position suitable for a visit, and it collapses upon the one who plays it.

what the former put into his philosophy and the latter into his verses, Aristophanes puts in the persons of Socrates and Euripides.

Comedy is the literary genre of the conservative parties. The distance between the tragic and the comic is the same as that which exists between wishing to be and believing that one already is. This is the step from the sublime to the ridiculous. The transference of the heroic character from the plane of will to that of perception causes the involution of tragedy, its disintegration—and makes comedy of it. The mirage appears as nothing but a mirage.

This happens with Don Quixote when, not content with affirming his desire for adventure, he persists in believing himself an adventurer. The immortal novel is in danger of becoming simply a comedy. The edge of a coin, as we have suggested, is all that separates the novel from pure comedy. The first readers of *Quixote* must have seen just comedy in this literary novelty. In the prologue of Avellaneda * the point is made twice: "Since the whole *Story of Don Quixote de la Mancha* is almost comedy," the above-mentioned prologue begins, and adds later: "Let him [Cervantes] be content with his *Galatea* and comedies in prose, for that is what most of his novels are." These phrases are not sufficiently explained by observing that the generic name of all theatrical work was *comedia* at that time.

* Author of an apocryphal Part II of *Don Quixote.* [Translators' note]

19

Tragicomedy

THE novelistic genre is, doubtless, comic. Let us not say humorous, because many vanities hide beneath the cloak of humor. First of all, it simply tries to make use of the poetic significance there is in the violent fall of the tragic figure, overcome by the force of inertia, by reality. When we talked of the realism of the novel we should have noted that there was something more than reality enclosed in that realism, something which allowed the latter to attain a poetic power which is so alien to it. Then it will become evident that the poetry of realism does not lie in inert reality but in the force of attraction which reality exercises over the metorlike ideals.

The upper level of the novel is a tragedy, from which the muse descends, following the tragic as it falls into comedy. The tragic line is inevitable, it must form part of the novel, if only as the very thin edge which limits it. For this reason, I believe that it is desirable to stick to the name found by Fernando de Rojas for his *Celestina:* tragicomedy. The novel is a tragicomedy. Perhaps in *La Celestina* the evolution of this genre reaches a climax, acquiring a maturity which finds its full expansion in *Quixote.* The tragic element, of course, may expand a great deal and even vie in scope and importance with the comic matter of the novel. All degrees and oscillations are possible here.

In the novel as a synthesis of tragedy and comedy, the strange desire hinted at by Plato without any comment

160

has been fulfilled. It was at the Banquet * in the early morning. The guests, overcome by the Dionysiac essence, lay dozing in confusion. Aristodemus awoke vaguely "when the roosters were already crowing." He seemed to see that only Socrates, Agathon, and Aristophanes remained awake. He thought he could hear them immersed in a difficult dialogue, in which Socrates argued against Agathon, the young author of tragedies, and Aristophanes, the comic writer, that the poet of tragedy and of comedy ought to be one and not two different men. This episode has not been satisfactorily explained but I have always suspected, when I read it, that Plato, a soul seething with intuitions, was planting here the seed of the novel. If we prolong the attitude taken by Socrates in the *Symposium* in the pale light of dawn, it will seem as if we come up against Don Quixote, the hero and the madman.

* Plato, *Symposium*. [Translators' note]

20

Flaubert, Cervantes, Darwin

THE sterility of what passes for patriotism in Spanish thought is made clear by the fact that the truly great Spanish accomplishments have not been studied sufficiently. Enthusiasm is wasted in sterile praise of what is not praiseworthy and cannot be applied with sufficient energy where it is most needed.

There is need of a book showing in detail that every novel bears *Quixote* within it like an inner filigree, in the same way as every epic poem contains the *Iliad* within it like the fruit its core. Flaubert is not reticent in proclaiming it: "Je retrouve," he says, "mes origines dans le livre que je savais par coeur avant de savoir lire, *Don Quichotte*." * Madame Bovary is a Don Quixote in skirts with a minimum of tragedy in her soul. She is a reader of romantic novels and a representative of the bourgeois ideals which have hovered over Europe for half a century. Wretched ideals! Bourgeois democracy, positivist romanticism!

Flaubert fully realizes that the novelistic art is a genre with critical intention and comic sinews: "Je tourne beaucoup à la critique," he writes at the time that he is composing *Bovary;* "le roman que j'écris m'aigüise cette faculté, car c'est une oeuvre surtout de critique ou plutôt d'anatomie." ** And in another place: "Ah! Ce qui manque à la société moderne ce n'est pas un Christ, ni un

* *Correspondance*, II, 16.
** *Ibid.*, 370.

Washington, ni un Socrate, ni un Voltaire, c'est un Aris-
tophane." * I believe that in matters of realism Flaubert
would not appear suspect and that he will be accepted as
an unimpeachable witness.

If the contemporary novel makes its comic mechanism
less obvious, it is due to the fact that the ideals attacked
by it are hardly removed from the reality with which
they are attacked. The tension is very weak: the ideal
falls from a very small height. For this reason it can be
predicted that the novel of the nineteenth century will be
unreadable very soon: it contains the least possible
amount of poetic dynamism. Even today we are surprised
that when a book of Daudet or of Maupassant *falls* into
our hands we do not feel the same pleasure that we felt
fifteen years ago, while the tension of *Don Quixote* promises never to slacken.

The ideal of the nineteenth century was realism. "Facts,
only facts," clamors a Dickensian character in *Hard
Times*. The how, not the why; the fact, not the idea,
preaches Auguste Comte. Madame Bovary breathes the
same air as M. Homais—a Comtist atmosphere. Flaubert
reads *La Philosophie positive* while he is writing his novel:
"C'est un ouvrage," he says "profondément farce; il faut
seulement lire, pour s'en convaincre, l'introduction qui en
est le résumé, il y a, pour quelqu'un qui voudrait faire
des charges au théâtre dans le goût aristophanesque, sur
les théories sociales, des californies de rires." **

Reality has such a violent temper that it does not tolerate the ideal even when reality itself is idealized. The
nineteenth century, not satisfied with raising the negation
of all heroism to a heroic form and enthroning the idea of
the positive, subjects this aim again to the ordeal of harsh
reality. Flaubert lets slip an extremely characteristic

* *Ibid.*, 159.
** *Loc. cit.*, II, 261.

phrase: "On me croit épris du réel, tandis que je l'exècre; car c'est en haine du réalisme que j'ai entrepris ce roman." *

These generations from which we are directly descended had taken a fatal stand. In *Quixote* the balance of poetic sensibility was already tipping towards the side of bitterness and it has not even in our day fully recovered. The nineteenth century, our parent, has felt a perverse delight in pessimism: it has wallowed in it, it has drunk it to the last drop and has compressed the world in such a way that nothing lofty could remain standing. A sort of gust of animosity is blown onto us by this whole century.

The natural sciences based on determinism conquered the field of biology during the first decades of the nineteenth century. Darwin believed he had succeeded in imprisoning life—our last hope—within physical necessity. Life is reduced to mere matter, physiology to mechanics. The human organism, which seemed an independent unit, capable of acting by itself, is placed in its physical environment like a figure in a tapestry. It is no longer the organism which moves but the environment which is moving through it. Our actions are no more than reactions. There is no freedom, no originality. To live is to adapt oneself; to adapt oneself is to allow the material environment to penetrate into us, to drive us out of ourselves. Adaptation is submission and renunciation. Darwin sweeps heroes off the face of the earth.

The hour of the "roman expérimental" arrives. Zola does not learn his poetry either from Homer or Shakespeare but from Claude Bernard. The subject matter is always man, but since man is no longer the agent of his acts but is moved by the environment in which he lives,

---

* *Correspondance*, III, 67–68. See what he writes on his *Dictionnaire des idées reçues:* Gustavus Flaubertus, Bourgeoisophobus.

the novel will look for the representation of the environment. The environment is the only protagonist. People speak of evoking the "atmosphere." Art submits to one rule: verisimilitude. But does not tragedy have its own internal independent verisimilitude? Is there not an esthetic *vero* or talisman—the beautiful—and a likeness of the beautiful? The answer is *no* according to positivism: the beautiful is what is probable and the true lies only in physics. The aim of the novel is physiology.

One night Bouvard and Pécuchet buried poetry in the Cemetery of Père Lachaise—in honor of verisimilitude and determinism.

Notes by Julián Marías

The following notes are those chosen by Julián Marías as the most essential from his complete Commentary to the Spanish edition of Ortega's *Meditaciones del Quijote*, Ediciones de la Universidad de Puerto Rico, Revista de Occidente, Madrid, 1957. References to *O.C.* indicate Ortega's *Obras completas*, vols. I–VI, Revista de Occidente, Madrid, 1946–47.

1. The theme of connection begins here. "Salvation" seeks the fullness of meaning, which is obtained by putting the theme "in direct relation with the elementary currents of the spirit, with the classic subjects of human preoccupation. Once it becomes interwoven with them it is transfigured, transubstantiated, saved." Love, connection, reason are the three converging elements in the constitution of philosophy. The idea of *"vital* reason" appears not long afterwards as the fitting expression of the intuition which is introduced in this context. (On "salvation," see the prologue to the book *Cinco salvaciones* [Five Salvations], by Francisco Maldonado Guevara, Madrid, 1953.)

2. From this point on, the references to love and its connection with philosophy are numerous. Love and perfection appear linked together in Spinoza too, but in a different form; for Spinoza, love is joy accompanied by the idea of its external cause, and joy is the transition of man to a greater perfection; it is a question, then, of the perfection of the *lover,* who, on becoming more perfect (and rejoicing) loves the cause of his perfection. For Ortega it is a question of the perfection of the *beloved object;* this perfection does not dwell "intrinsically" in the beloved object, but each object must come out of itself to reach perfection, to enter into connection with the other objects: "Each thing is a fairy whose inner treasures are concealed beneath poor commonplace garments, a virgin who has to be loved to become fruitful." The transfiguration or salvation of a theme consists in connecting it with the motives of our preoccupation, with the elementary currents of our spirit.
166

Therefore, Ortega proposes "a doctrine of love," since "love binds us to things, even if only temporarily." "The beloved object is, to begin with, that which seems indispensable to us." The beloved object is then a "part of ourselves," and consequently, there is in love "an extension of the individuality which absorbs other things into it, which unites them to us." But this is not the end of the matter: when this link or connection gives full reality to the beloved object and uncovers its virtualities (remember Ortega's "reflections"), it reveals it to us in all its depth and worth; and then we discover the connections of the beloved object, not only with us, but with other things to which it is bound, and therefore with us too. Hence the *universal* connection which love builds and establishes what one might call its "world-building" character. Let us not forget that the image of Jericho (discussed later) is essential in Ortega's methodology: he is using here one of those concentric circles, the widest one, with which to encircle and hem in what, in his maturity, will be the notion of "human life" as it appears from the viewpoint of *vital* reason.

3. In this passage Ortega outlines a first statement of his ethical thought, negatively and positively. It could be systematized in the following way: 1. Immoralism is absurd, it lacks common sense; the reason for this constitutes the nucleus of Ortega's theory of ethics: human life is *intrinsically* moral, morality is its very nature, not a luxury or something extra. 2. The greatest enemies of the moral idea are, however, the perverse moralities, in which the very character of morality is perverted. 3. Among them are included all utilitarian moralities. 4. Utilitarianism affects moralities which in themselves are not utilitarian in character, if they are applied in a utilitarian way; that is, if their concrete realization in the in-dividual man is utilitarian. 5. Morality does not consist in rigidity; the opposite is usually the case: rigidity is frequently the disguise of hypocrisy (as illustrated by Pharisaism). 6. For centuries now, an effort has been made to refine and purify the ethical ideal, "mak-ing it more and more delicate and complex, more crystalline and more intimate." 7. One essential result of this effort is the distinc-tion between goodness and "the material observance of legal rules which have been adopted once and for all"; the only moral person is the one who "tries, before any new action, to renew immediate contact with the ethical value itself." Compare this with the dis-tinction that might be made from the Christian point of view be-tween merely "not breaking the commandments" and actually "keeping" them: a non-Christian who does not steal or lie, ob-viously does not break the respective commandments, but it would make no sense to say that he keeps them, just as the Christian does not observe the precepts of other religions although his conduct may coincide with them. A commandment is kept only when con-

duct conforms to it *through love of God,* that is when the conduct derives from the first commandment. For the Christian an act is only *moral in a Christian way* when it is derived from an "immediate contact with the ethical value itself," which in this case is literally the person of Christ. 8. Morality needs to be constantly vivified, ever reviewing its motives, and therefore it must be "open," ready for reform, correction, and expansion. It is a characteristic comparable to that of philosophical certainty, which must be constantly proving itself, that is, making itself evident. 9. The field of morality is wide open, and man must explore it, as he explores nature. 10. To the perverse and closed morality is opposed the integral morality "for which understanding is a clear and primary duty," and in it is concentrated "a true religious attitude," the affirmative opening to reality.

4. In 1932 Ortega writes: "*I am myself plus my circumstance.* This expression which appears in my first book and which condenses all my philosophic thought . . ." But this does not mean, of course, that the truth of a philosophy is contained *in* that or any other similar expression. Ortega adds that the twelve hundred pages of Hegel's *Logik* are a preparation for bringing out the full meaning of the sentence "The idea is the absolute"; in other words, that this expression has no meaning without them. The proposition which sums up a philosophy is not separable from the totality of the philosophy, but its mission is "to liberate" the intellective energy accumulated in the whole doctrine. Ortega's philosophy is not contained *in* the thesis "I am myself plus my circumstance," but that sentence can only be understood when it serves as a condensation of that philosophy as a whole and its formulation brings this doctrine suddenly into focus, thus making possible its true comprehension.

5. The fundamental idea of circumstance as a condition of human life had already originated in Ortega's thought independently of and previous to the stimuli of Uexküll and Husserl. In the extraordinary essay "Adán en el Paraíso" (*Adam in Paradise*) (1910) which exposes in a very closely knit and coherent form, although with less conceptual precision, the nucleus of what would become Ortega's philosophy, we find some ideas which are the immediate antecedent of the *Meditations on Quixote:* "Take any kind of object, apply to it different systems of evaluation, and you will have as many other different objects instead of a single one. Compare what the earth is for a farmer and for an astronomer: the farmer is satisfied with treading the reddish surface of the planet and scratching it with the plough; his earth is a road, some furrows, and a grain field. The astronomer needs to determine exactly the place that the globe occupies at each instant within the vast

supposition of sidereal space; from the standpoint of exactness he is forced to convert it into a mathematical abstraction, into a case of universal gravitation. The examples could be continued indefinitely; therefore, there is no such thing as a changeless and unique reality with which to compare the contents of artistic works: there are as many realities as there are viewpoints. The point of view creates the panorama. There is an everyday reality formed by a system of loose, approximate, vague relationships which is sufficient for the purpose of daily living. There is a scientific reality formed by a system of exact relationships, a system which the need for exactness imposes" (*O.C.*, I, 471). "When Adam appeared in Paradise, like a new tree, this thing we call life began to exist. What then is Adam, with the verdure of Paradise *around him, surrounded* by animals, the rivers with their restless fish there in the distance and farther away the mountains with their petrified insides, and then the seas and other lands, and the Earth and the worlds?" (*ibid.*, 476). And finally: "Adam in Paradise. Who is Adam? Anyone and no one in particular: life. Where is Paradise? The landscape of the North or of the South? It does not matter: it is the ubiquitous *stage* for the immense tragedy of living" (*ibid.*, 489; the italics are mine). (See my commentary on this essay by Ortega in "Algunas precisiones sobre la filosofía de Ortega" [Some points on Ortega's philosophy], *Leonardo*, vol. III, Barcelona, 1945; also collected under the title "Vida y razón en la filosofía de Ortega" [Life and reason in Ortega's philosophy] in my book *Filosofía actual y existencialismo en España* [Present-day philosophy and Existentialism in Spain]).

Finally, the expression "circumstances" appears explicitly in an article of Ortega's dated January, 1911, "Vejamen del orador" [Criticism of the orator], and with a general sense which anticipates the passage from the *Meditations* we are commenting upon here: "What are *circumstances?* Are they only these hundred people, these fifty minutes, this little question? Every circumstance is enclosed in a broader one. Why think that I am only surrounded by ten metres of space? What about those beyond these ten? What a serious oversight, what wretched stupidity it is to take into account but a few circumstances when *in reality everything surrounds us!* I do not sympathize with the madman and the mystic: My enthusiasm is for the man who takes circumstances into account *provided that he forgets none*" (*O.C.*, I, 557; the italics are mine). These words seem to be connected with those which introduce this concept in the *Meditations:* "Man reaches his full capacity when he acquires complete consciousness of his circumstances. Through them he communicates with the universe."

The stylistic devices with which Ortega introduces this concept should be emphasized: first, the use of exclamation marks; second, the use of the word in the singular—rather uncommon in Spanish. The latter is a stylistic device which attracts attention to a word and gives a special shade to its meaning; thus, Ortega frequently says "*la* tiniebla" [the shadows], "*el* Alpe" [the Alps]. In the present instance, the intention is to avoid the triviality with which this word is often used and which is reflected in the Academy Dictionary definition, and to give to it the fullness of its meaning. For that reason he takes it in its literal Latin sense, and with the value of a neuter plural: *circum-stantia:* "The mute things which are all around us!" The circumstance is all that surrounds us, what is *circum me*, around me, surrounding me. It is a purely *functional* concept, which does not prejudge anything but takes reality in all its immediacy and purity; in this sense, it is much more radical than *Umwelt* [the world around]. Ortega's description adds immediately a few intensely interesting notes: the *mute* things raise their *silent* faces; that is, the circumstance has no voice or meaning—we shall see presently the scope of this. Yet neither is it a question of an inert or passive "being there," since things are an *offering* and a *gift*. We are oriented towards something and images are accumulated to show this: our eyes are fixed on remote enterprises, we are projected, the hero advances like an *arrow* towards a *goal*. With the initial character of an offering and a project, Ortega introduces the dialogue between circumstantial reality and the self whose circumstance it is.

6. The first thing that Ortega says about perspective is that it is the ultimate reality of the world; that is, he does not attribute it primarily to knowledge nor to any of its aspects, but to *the real*. He does not imply that matter and spirit are not real, but that they are not the *ultimate* reality of the world, because this reality is "no definite thing." This takes us miles away from any "subjectivism," from any reduction of the real to the person who looks at it. It is just the opposite: a reality with its own precise structure which has to be reckoned with to reach the truth. When he adds that "God is perspective and hierarchy; Satan's sin was an error of perspective," he takes the opposite attitude to that of Nietzsche when the latter tries to put himself *jenseits von Wahr und Falsch* [beyond the true and false]. He adds also that "perspective is perfected by the multiplication of its viewpoints and the precision with which we react to each one of its planes." Whenever a particular point of view is set up as absolute, instead of putting it in its proper place within the total perspective, one makes the error of usurping God's point of view (if the expression may be allowed), which is none other than the infinity of all possible viewpoints, the integration of all perspectives. That is the basis for saying that all claims of "the absolutism of intellect," of affirmation of a particular system to the exclusion of all others, are forms

—no matter how innocuous in intention—of "Satanism."
In "Verdad y perspectiva" [Truth and perspective], less than
two years after the *Meditations*, Ortega turns back to this subject
in greater detail: "Reality, just because it is reality and exists outside of our individual minds, can only reach us by multiplying
itself into a thousand faces or surfaces." "Reality cannot be observed except from the point of view to which each of us has
been inescapably assigned in the universe. That reality and this
point of view are correlative, and just as reality cannot be invented, so the point of view cannot be feigned either." "Truth,
the real, the universe, life—whatever you want to call it—breaks
down into innumerable facets, into countless planes, each one of
which slants towards one individual. If the latter has known how
to be faithful to his own point of view, if he has resisted the eternal
temptation to exchange his retina for an imaginary one, what he
sees will be a real aspect of the world." "And vice versa: each
man has a mission of truth. My eye has its unique place: the part
of reality that my eye sees is seen by no other eye. We are irreplaceable, we are necessary." "Reality, then, appears in individual
perspectives. What for one is in the background, exists in the
foreground for another. The landscape arranges its sizes and distances in accordance with our retina, and our heart apportions
the emphasis. Visual and intellectual perspectives are further complicated by the perspective of evaluation" (*O.C.*, II, 18–19). To
follow the developments of the idea of perspective in Ortega
would lead to a complete exposition of his philosophy. It can be
seen, especially in the final chapter of *El tema de nuestro tiempo*
[*The Modern Theme*] (1923), entitled "La doctrina del punto de
vista" [The Doctrine of the Point of View], and its appendix on
"El sentido histórico de la teoría de Einstein" [The Historical
Significance of the Theory of Einstein], especially its Chapter 2,
"Perspectivismo" [Perspectivism], in which he defines "provincial-
ism" or the "provincial spirit" as an optical error by virtue of
which the individual does not recognize his off-center position and
believes that he is in the center of the globe. Ortega recalls that
"Truth and Perspective" appeared before Einstein had published
Die Grundlage der allgemeinen Relativitätstheorie, the first book
about the general theory of relativity. In *The Modern Theme*
Ortega simply develops and formulates with greater precision the
idea that we have considered. His more precise formula is this:
"Cosmic reality is such that it can only be seen under a definite
perspective. *Perspective is one of the components of reality*. Far
from being its deformation it is its organization. A reality which
would remain always the same when seen from different points is
an absurdity" (*O.C.*, III, 199). "This way of thinking leads to a
radical reform of philosophy and, what is more important, of our
cosmic sensation" (*ibid.*, 200). And when referring to the "ab-

solute" vision, he observes that the sum total of individual perspectives—omniscience, the true "absolute reason"—"is the sublime function which we attribute to God. God is also a point of view; but not because He possesses an observatory beyond the human sphere which makes Him see universal reality directly, as if He were an old rationalist. God is not a rationalist. His point of view is that of each one of us; *our partial truth is also truth for God.* To such an extent our perspective is true and our reality authentic! But God, as the catechism says, is everywhere, so that He enjoys all points of view and in His limitless vitality gathers together and harmonizes all our horizons" (*ibid.*, 202–203). This, incidentally, is what some people usually call "subjectivism" and "relativism."

The conclusive idea, as is apparent, is that for Ortega *perspective is one of the components of reality,* that is, its organization and not its deformation. The word "reality" lacks meaning for us outside of the perspective in which it is constituted and organized, that is, in which it is *real.* We might say that *reality as such only exists as a perspective.* (Cf. Note 26.)

7. In my opinion this passage—one of the decisive ones in all Ortega's work—has never been adequately understood and has scarcely been noticed. On the other hand, its difficulty cannot be denied. It deals with the *concrete* destiny of man, not with the destiny of man in general—*die Bestimmung des Menschen* in Fichte's sense, for example; and this concrete destiny is, says Ortega, the reabsorption of circumstance, that is to say, the circumstance of each individual. Man, the hero, he has already said, "goes forward, impetuous and straight as an arrow towards a glorious goal"; we go "projected" towards distant places; and circumstance asks us to accept its "offering." The reabsorption of the circumstance consists in its humanization, in its incorporation into that project of man. Man makes himself *with the things which are offered to him,* makes life out of them, his own life, he assumes them by projecting on them that sense, that *logos* or significance about which he speaks a little later. The destiny of man, when he is faithful to his situation, that is, his *concrete* destiny, is to impose his personal project on what is real, to give sense to that which has none, to extract the *logos* from the inert, brutish and "il-logical," to convert that which simply "is there around me" (circumstance) into a real *world,* into *personal human life.* Not only is this interpretation not capricious, not only does it not do violence to the texts, but it would have easily been reached if the *Meditations* had been read carefully as a whole, without separating the first part from the second, and taking what is said there seriously. Actually the passage we are commenting upon here is inseparable from another at the end of the book which says: "Since the character of the heroic lies in the *will to*

be what one is not yet, half of the figure of the tragic protagonist *is outside of reality.* It is sufficient to pull him by the feet and restore him completely to reality, for him to become a comic character. The noble heroic fiction *rises above the inertia of reality* through the greatest exertions; it lives by *aspiration. The future* is its witness. The *vis comica* simply accentuates the inclination of the hero towards pure materiality. *Reality advances* through the fiction, imposes itself on us and *reabsorbs the tragic role.* The hero made this role part of himself, he fused himself with it. *The reabsorption by reality consists in solidifying, in materializing the aspiring intention of the hero upon his person.*" (p. 158) He deals here with the reverse question, the reabsorption of man —of the project—*by circumstance.* Reality, which does not allow itself to be easily dominated, which to a certain extent is irreducible —man is a utopian being, Ortega says later—advances and more or less solidifies, materializes the aspiring intention. In other words, while man tries to "humanize," personalize circumstance, reality treats man as a thing, solidifies him and so deprives him of his disposition to invention and aspiration, the most genuinely human attribute. This is the authentic human condition: the unattainable, ever-renewed enterprise which consists in *living,* in trying to be a human being. (Compare note 36.)

8. This is the most compressed formula of Ortega's fundamental intuition. As we see, he enunciates in a conceptual and precise form what he had expressed metaphorically four years earlier in "Adam in Paradise." But it must be noted at this point that circumstance is not to be understood only in a geographical way, nor in a physical way generally, nor even in a merely organic way. It is sufficient to recall what he says later on (p. 85): "The external world! But is not the imperceptible world—the deeper zones—also external to the ego? There is no doubt that it is external and it is so in a very high degree." That is to say, the imperceptible, the so-called "inner" world, is external to the individual, to the "myself" of the expression we are commenting upon, therefore, it forms part of the circumstance. It can only be said that it forms part of *me* in the sense of the first "I," that which designates my whole personal reality. Perhaps it is not out of place to recall a former commentary of mine on this passage of Ortega's: "The *self* aspect of man—the *myself* in Ortega's sentence—does not exhaust the human entity as idealism believed. But we are now more interested in the first 'I,' the one which includes the circumstance and is not merely the *self* who lives, the *center* of a *circumstantia.* Circumstance, in fact, is defined by its being around—*circum*—a self. It is this self that gives it its unitary and circumstantial character, that is, its vitality; but we cannot now define the self simply by the circumstance as the central

point of the latter. The self is inseparable from the circumstance and has no meaning aside from it; but, conversely, the circumstance only exists around a self, and not just any self, a mere subject who performs acts and deeds, but an "I myself," capable of introspection which is not *something*—that is a thing, *res*—but *someone*, a person. We could say that I am defined by my circumstance, but that my circumstance does not define me; which means that I exist only within it, and that it determines my being, but does not exhaust it. My being, or rather, my future being, is not simply the combination of my circumstance and an abstract, pointlike 'I' as its subjective center. The circumstance is *my* circumstance, and this possessive does not indicate a simple location, but an actual possession. Because I am myself, because I have a 'selfness' and am master of myself, I can have something of *my own*. The self does not include all of man, but neither does mere *subjectivity*—by which I do not mean immanence but the function of being the subject who confronts objective reality. The self is not a mere support or substratum of the circumstance; it is not an impersonal *one who* lives with it, but a personal *he who* lives, who makes his life with the circumstance. Man, besides being a self and the subject who performs his vital actions, the support of his world, is also a *person*" (*Miguel de Unamuno*, 1943, Chapter III, Section "Existencia y persona" [Existence and person]).

On the fundamental meaning of the "I," and therefore, the ultimate character of human life, Ortega does not give specific details in this passage, and it might seem as if these points do not arise at this level of his thought; but farther on we shall see that specific references to these questions are to be found in this book. The expression "if I do not save it (the circumstance) I cannot save myself" contains the *philosophical* reason for Ortega's choice of Spain as a theme and also the justification of patriotism in general.

9. Ortega begins in this passage a peculiar type of intellectual approach to an object which is also peculiar. These pages represent an essential innovation in method, the first sample of what is to be the very nucleus of Ortega's philosophy: the method of *vital* reason. As often occurs, the method is put into practice before being formulated, simply because it can only be established through practice as in the case of phenomenology, begun in [Husserl's] *Logische Untersuchungen* [Investigations in Logic] and formulated theoretically only in his *Ideen zur einer reinen Phänomenologie* [Ideas: general introduction to pure phenomenology]. In my aforementioned essay (see Note 5) many years ago, I dealt with this "vital description," which corresponds to the discovery of an object which might be called "the lived-in forest," that is, the forest not as a "thing," but as a concrete reality

rooted in my life. All the rest are abstractions, abstract interpretations (viewed as things) of what a wood basically and authentically is. From Heidegger's theory of *Zuhandensein* [existing nearby]
as opposed to *Vorhandensein* [existence], to the "Existential"
descriptions which can be found in the works of Sartre and his
disciples, we are confronted with ways of access to the real whose
antecedent—more mature, incidentally, and better adapted to
reality—is this passage from the *Meditations on Quixote*. What
Ortega shows is, above all, that in the description of the forest
I necessarily enter, and without reference to *me* that description
is not possible. The reason for this is that *without me there is no
forest*. Does this mean that the forest is a "subjective" reality?
Not at all: the forest is something perfectly real and "objective,"
something which exists "outside of me," so much outside that I
am "in" the forest. Am I then "part" of the forest? Not that
either, because this would mean to consider both the forest and
myself as "things." What does not exist nor have sense is the
forest "in itself," neither "in itself"—realism—nor "in me"—idealism. Actually, Ortega's philosophical innovation consists above all
(both as a principle and as a method) in going beyond those two
forms of "thing-making" thinking—whether the objects thought
of are material objects or the mind that thinks—the two forms
on which a philosophy believed by some to be the last word (but
which is, as we see, the last but one) falls back anachronistically.
The forest is something real, distinct from me, with which and in
which I find myself, without its being identified with me; but the
supposed forest has no reality "in itself"; it needs me in order *to
be;* that is, to be itself, to be *the said forest*. My possibilities *as
such* in the face of a portion of reality, of what there is, constitute
the being of the forest. We shall see this in further details of our
commentary.

10. Ortega gives the name of "patent world" to that part of reality
which is revealed without any effort except that of opening our
eyes, that is, to the world "of mere impressions." Now that "world"
is not the *world* which includes essentially the *transworld* of
structures—latent in the former—which requires effort and intervention on our part; but this, he goes on, "neither adds to nor
detracts from the reality of that world." "World" and "transworld," that is, the mere impressions which invade us and the
structures which we, in the process of living, introduce, as we
interpret those impressions, make up the real *world* in which we
live.

11. The purely passive way of seeing would not give us a world
but only a chaos of bright dots; the active seeing or observing—
the only real *seeing—is* interpretation. The relation between the

two is reciprocal and necessary: there is no interpretation without vision nor vision without interpretation; that is, vision—perception in general—is interpretative, and interpretation is perceptive. For that reason Ortega says in his later writings that what we call "things" are interpretations of the real, and hence his idea of *being* as something which man makes with what *there is* and of man as a world-maker. Ortega is referring to the Platonic concept of *idea*.

12. Ortega calls foreshortening the surface which, without ceasing to be a surface, expands in depth; that is, it is the confluence of the materiality of a surface (the aspect under which it is merely superficial) with a second latent life, consisting in the fact that a certain depth is present in it. Let us not forget that nothing can "present" itself except by becoming superficial or patent. When this occurs, the surface functions in these two senses, that is, as *manifestation of the latent*, as a presence which points at and declares its hidden depth. "Vision in depth is made possible by foreshortening, in which we find an extreme case of a fusion of simple vision with a purely intellectual act." This concept of foreshortening is particularly important, because it contains the two sides of perception or, one might say, of intellection. Foreshortening is at the same time both vision and what is seen. *Reality is seen in foreshortening*, that is, in perspective, and this means: (a) concretely (since the point of view is always this one and no other); (b) intellectively (through a certain interpretation); but, on the other hand, *reality is foreshortening*, meaning that it is constituted and forced upon me as soon as it manifests itself and exists for me in perspective. I believe that this notion of foreshortening contains possibilities not yet exploited even remotely. Undoubtedly it is taken from the visual sphere, but it should be noted (1) that Ortega takes the idea in its fullest scope and therefore makes clear that the dimension of depth appears in a surface (therefore in foreshortening), "whether of space or time, whether visual or aural," and it would be necessary to elaborate the theory of "analogical" forms or, one might say, "homologous" forms of foreshortening; (2) that the visual interpretation is given justified primacy, since sight is the sense with which we apprehend "world-hood" or the world as such (on this, see my article "La interpretación visual del mundo" [The visual interpretation of the world] in *La Nación*, Buenos Aires, March 18, 1956).

13. The theory of structure which begins with these words deserves to be examined carefully, because there are in it a number of innovations which have, perhaps, been fruitful in recent philosophy. Ortega understands "structure" as a peculiar "reality," as a "thing in a secondary sense," resulting from adding to the simple

elements something different from them, namely, an *order*. The latter is, as Ortega emphasizes, quite distinct from the former insofar as its kind of reality is concerned: "It is evident that the *reality* of that order has a value or significance different from the *reality possessed by its elements*" (the italics are mine). "It is this interlocking of things that forms a structure," he adds. That is, it is not a question of there being "things" or "elements" arranged in certain structures. What Ortega calls structure is a *reality* which *includes* the elements in a certain order, combination or relationship. We could formulate it thus: elements + order = structure. The result is that the "thing" by itself alone—the *bare* element—has very little *reality:* "How unimportant a thing would be if it were only what it is in isolation?" "One might say that they love each other and aspire to unite, to collect in communities, in organisms, in structures, in worlds." The effective realities are structures in which arrangements or combinations of different value or significance are superimposed on the material elements. The culmination of it is *Nature* as such: *"What we call 'Nature' is only the maximum structure into which all material elements have entered."* It is the superior organization—that is, that of the highest "order"—and at the same time that in which all material elements enter, not just some of them. In the hierarchy of structures of material elements, Nature is the superior one, and those realities which, seen from the *simple* elements, are already "structures" (organisms, societies, etc.), function as "elements" of it.

The matter does not end here, however. Things cannot be taken in their isolation, as we have already seen. In the visual field, first confused and disorderly, "gradually order sets in"; our attention begins to spread "a net of relationships" between things. There is nothing subjective in this however; we are dealing with the very structure of the real: "A thing cannot be focused or confined except with others." It is not that I "set up" arbitrary relationships on my own account; the decisive factor is the *discovery of reflections* and connections of things *in* the thing being considered: "If we continue paying attention to one object, it will become more clearly perceived because we shall keep finding in it more reflections of the connections with the surrounding things." This is what Ortega calls "depth": "And this is what the depth of something means: what there is in it of reflection of other things, allusion to other things. The reflection is the most apparent form in which one thing virtually exists in another." Depth and *reflection* are seen as virtual existence of one thing in another, that is the *tangible* form—and therefore metaphorical too —of the structure, as is the case with the word "perspective." When Ortega proclaims the perspectivistic character of reality itself, when he says that perspective, far from being the deformation of reality, is its organization, he only expresses in another form the idea that reality is fundamentally *structure*, irreducible to *mere* elements, since the order or disposition of these elements has to be added to them, and that order consists in the virtual existence of some elements *in* others, with *reflection* as its apparent symbol. "The 'meaning' of a thing," he concludes, "is the highest form of its coexistence with other things, it is its depth dimension. No, it is not enough for me to have the material body of a thing; I *need*, besides, to know its 'meaning,' that is to say, the mystic shadow which the rest of the universe casts on it" (italics are mine).

14. This paragraph is the prelude to a decisive piece of Ortegan philosophy. Concept and limit appear as "new virtual things," essentially different from the material things; their mission is not to "duplicate" the latter, even less to supplant them, but to "interpolate and interject themselves" among them. The affinity of these expressions with "interpretation" is evident. The mission of these "schematic natures" (*skhêma* is figure, configuration) is "to mark the borders of beings," to keep the realities together but distinct, in coexistence but without confusion. And that is the *concept*. In 1929, he says: "Things by themselves have no measure, they are incommensurate, they are neither more nor less, neither this way nor the other; in short, they neither are nor are not. The measure of things, their character, their being just so much or just such a way and not any other, is what constitutes their *being* and this being implies the intervention of man." And in order that the connection with the idea of limits may be clearer, he adds in a note: "Cardinal Cusano made profound puns by deriving *mensura* from *mens*" (*O.C.*, IV, 58). Later in 1933 he says that man "mobilizes his mental faculties by drawing up a plan of self-orientation with regard to each thing and to the totality of things or universe. This plan of self-orientation is what we call the being of things" (*O.C.*, V, 87–88).

15. This ill-humored reference to *irrationalism* gives the other half of Ortega's point of view. Irrationalism had already had a long history; in fact it began with the discovery of the realities—life, history—which, because they are interesting in themselves, because they are *irreducible*, do not admit of *explanation* (cf. "La razón en la filosofía actual" [Reason in present-day philosophy], in my *Ensayos de teoría*. This attitude, which had been gradually developing since Kierkegaard, was to reappear, in different forms, in Nietzsche and William James, in Bergson and in Unamuno. "The same is true of existence as of movement," Kierkegaard wrote, "it is very difficult to apprehend. If I think about them, I annul them, and therefore, I do not think about them. So it might seem correct to say that there is something which does not allow of thought:

existence. But then the difficulty remains that because the one who thinks exists, existence is posited at the same time as thought" (*concluding Unscientific Postscript*, 2nd part, 2nd section, Chapter III, § 1). In Bergson the idea appears with still greater precision, in a series of theses which he comments upon and develops throughout all his work: *"Our intelligence, as it leaves nature's hands, has unorganized matter as its principal object"* (*L'Evolution créatrice*, p. 166–167). *"Intelligence sees clearly only the discontinuous"* (p. 168). "Let us limit ourselves to saying that the stable and immovable are the things to which our intelligence attaches itself in virtue of its natural disposition. *Our intelligence only sees immobility clearly"* (p. 169). "We are only at our ease in the discontinuous, in the motionless, in death. *Intelligence is characterized by a natural incomprehension of life"* (p. 179). But the closest to this idea was Unamuno, who in 1912 had written his book *Del sentimiento trágico de la vida* [*The Tragic Sense of Life*] (*in men and in peoples* was added on the cover of his first Spanish edition). In this book, thrilling, irritating, and brilliant, penetrating and irresponsible, Unamuno, although his last *intuition* might perhaps have led him along other paths, gave irrationalism its most energetic, intense and passionate expression, and possibly its happiest: "For living is one thing and knowing another, and, as we shall see, perhaps there is between them such opposition that we might say that *everything vital is not only irrational but anti-rational, and everything rational, anti-vital*. And this is the basis of the tragic sense of life" (p. 38). "Actually *reason is the enemy of life*.—Intelligence is a terrible thing. It tends toward death as memory towards stability. What is alive, what is absolutely unstable, absolutely individual, is, strictly speaking, unintelligible. Logic tends to reduce everything to identities and types, so that each representation may have only a single and identical content in any place, time or relation in which it occurs for us. And there is nothing which is the same during two successive moments of its existence. My idea of God is different each time I conceive it. *Identity, which is death, is the aspiration of the intellect. The mind seeks the dead, for the living escapes it;* it wants to stop the running waters and turn them into icy blocks, to 'pin them down.' In order to analyse a body, it must be diminished or destroyed. *In order to understand something one must kill it,* make it rigid in the mind. . . . *How, then, can reason be opened to the revelation of life?* It is a tragic struggle, it is the essence of tragedy, *the struggle of life with reason.* And truth? Does one live or does one comprehend?" (p. 92). And again: *"Everything vital is irrational, and everything rational is anti-vital,* because reason is essentially skeptical" (p. 93). Finally, after having insisted that, in spite of everything, faith, which is life, and reason have a mutual need of each other, he concludes: "Nevertheless, neither is faith transmissible or rational, *nor is reason vital*" (p. 115; I quote from the first edition, which Ortega could have known when writing the *Meditations;* the italics are mine. Cf. my book, *Miguel de Unamuno,* especially Chapter II).

Ortega was writing in this philosophical situation, and in this particular Spanish intellectual circumstance. It does not seem to me too venturesome to conjecture that *The Tragic Sense* was a polemical stimulus for Ortega, which forced him perhaps to mature his incipient theory of *vital* reason in order to oppose that attractive, fascinating formulation of irrationalism. For that purpose, Ortega had to deal with the problem at a more profound level, from which it could be seen that, *in view of the generally accepted idea of reason,* irrationalism was justified and reasonable, but that such an idea of reason was entirely insufficient. Ortega, then, had to go beyond irrationalism, but not in order to fall back on rationalism, as *opposed to which the former was right,* but to go beyond both, to reason in its full and precise form of *vital reason.*

16. Coming after all the previous chapters, this consideration is like an aeroplane "looping the loop," as Ortega enjoyed saying. The instrumental character of the concept is linked up now with the "tactical turn" aimed at taking possession of the concrete, which was seen earlier. That seizure, that possession, is the form in which security is obtained. And the basic human form of security is the *clarity* with which the "meaning" or *logos* of things appears, thus arranging the latter in a *context,* in a system of realities, that is, interpreting them. It is the double meaning of the expression "to know what we have to reckon with," which includes, besides the aspect of security (what we have to reckon with), that of clarity (to know); it is a security which *consists in clarity.* The culmination of it all is the formula, already quoted, of the mature Ortega, according to which *being* is the *plan of self-orientation* with respect to things, that *interpretation* which allows us to know "what we have to reckon with" concerning the real, concerning *what exists,* and what we have *to cope with, by accounting* for it.

17. It would be difficult to find a more energetic, categorical and insistent formulation than this. The title of this chapter is "Light as an Imperative," and this passage is the central nucleus which makes that title. It is at the same time the reason for the interpretation of truth as *aletheia* which Ortega has taken up before (cf. Chapter 4, *Worlds Beyond*). Let it be remembered that *before* introducing the concept of truth, Ortega had referred to the sudden "illumination" which he has at its discovery. Now the justification of the idea that "truth" is a discovery or *revelation*

is that the mission of man, the one which belongs to him *intrinsically*, without external imposition or possible escape, that which he is *constitutionally* and *basically* ("the very *root* of his *constitution*") is none other than *clarity*. To be a man is to illuminate, to clarify, to throw light on things, and thus "to discover them," to make them patent, to make them *true*. "Truths, once known," Ortega had written before (Chapter 4), "acquire a utilitarian *crust; they* no longer interest us *as truths* but as useful recipes." That is to say, they cease being truths *sensu stricto,* since they become "covered" by a *crust* (an energetic and plastic expression), they change into something which is handled in a utilitarian way, without clarity or expressiveness. It should be observed that *this is not all,* and that the deepest stratum of this thought will only appear a little farther on, and with it the real justification of the preceding.)

A comparison with some passages from Heidegger in *Sein und Zeit* is opportune at this point. In Chapter 28 Heidegger refers to the "ontologically figurative way of speaking" about the *lumen naturale* in man, which, according to him, means nothing else but "the ontological-existential structure" of *Dasein* [existence]; his "illuminated or clarified being" means "illuminated in itself *as* being-in-the-world, not through another entity, but in such a way that the being itself *is* the illumination." Only to an entity thus illuminated existentially, he adds, does the present (*Vorhandenes*) become accessible in the light, hidden in darkness. And he concludes that the *Dasein* or existence is its *Erschlossenheit*, its opening or disclosure (*Sein und Zeit*, p. 133). In Chapter 44, "*Dasein, Erschlossenheit und Wahrheit,*" Heidegger refers to the passage which I have just quoted and observes that "only with the *Erschlossenheit* or disclosure of the *Dasein* does one reach the *most basic* phenomenon of truth" [*Wahrheit*]. "Insofar as the *Dasein* essentially *is* its disclosure, something disclosed which discloses and discovers, it is essentially 'true.' *The Dasein is 'in the truth.'*" And he adds that this thesis has ontological meaning, that "the opening up of its most characteristic being belongs to its existential constitution" (*ibid.*, p. 221). On these theses is based Heidegger's whole derivation from the "truth," which he had previously taken from the Hellenic notion of *aletheia*, and the consequence that "there is truth only insofar as and as long as there is *Dasein*" (*ibid.*, p. 226), and that all truth, as regards its existential character, is relative to the being of the *Dasein* (*ibid.*, p. 227). This is the most profound and probably most fertile nucleus of Heidegger's philosophy.

18. From this point of view, the genres "are wide vistas seen from the main sides of human nature"; that is, the different *dimensions* of man, his basic possibilities, which are tendencies or directions,

acquire a certain actuality, a manifestation or visibility, in the different genres. The latter, far from being mere conventions, are explications of fundamental aspects of what is human, and in their own way they constitute, we might say, an "anthropology." The word is not in the text but the idea is. Ortega adds that "each epoch brings with it a basic interpretation of man," and he corrects his expression by saying that "the epoch does not bring the interpretation with it but actually *is* such an interpretation"; this is the reason that each epoch prefers a particular genre. Each epoch *is* an interpretation of man, and one of the fundamental ways in which that interpretation *is carried out* and realized is the most genuine genre, the one that the epoch creates—or re-creates. The *historic* nature of literary genres, which are not an abstract and intemporal world of "forms" and "rules," makes the "anthropology" which they create *concrete* also, a manifestation and temporal unfolding of the "main dimensions," of the basic tendencies which constitute man.

19. This passage is especially important. It is stated tentatively and not without some hesitation: "perhaps we should find"; doubtless Ortega perceived how daring this thought was. The point is that we do not consider real *what actually happens,* but a certain manner of happening that *is familiar to us.* He adds expressions still more surprising: not so much what is *seen* as *foreseen;* not so much what we *see* as what we *know.* "And if a series of *events* takes an *unforeseen* turn, we say it seems *incredible.*" All this is disconcerting: what happens, what is seen, what we see is disqualified as "real"; and the familiar, the foreseen, what we know, is contrasted with it; and if what happens is contrary to our expectations, it seems incredible to us. This means that before anything happened, before we saw anything, we were already on a *deeper plane of reality,* from which we spontaneously and radically disqualify as incredible what exists before us, what is *actually* happening. In other words, previously *we were counting on* reality, we possessed it beforehand, we literally foresaw it. This is simply the discovery of that stratum of human life which Ortega later calls *beliefs.* A careful reading of the study *Ideas y creencias* [Ideas and beliefs], written in 1934, published in 1940, will show that it is only the maturity of this seed, as the following sentences indicate: "Everything we think about acquires for us *ipso facto* a problematic reality and occupies in our lives a secondary place if it is compared with our genuine beliefs. We do not think about the latter either now or later; our relation with them consists in something much more efficient: counting on them, always, unceasingly" (*O.C.,* V, 381-382). "Beliefs constitute the basis of our lives, the ground on which they take place, because they put before us what to us is reality itself" (*ibid.,* 383). "On the

other hand, ideas, that is, the thoughts we have about things, whether original or acquired, do not possess the value of reality in our lives" (*ibid.*, 384). "The highest truth is that of the self-evident, but the value of the self-evident itself is, in its turn, mere theory, idea, and intellectual fabrication" (*ibid.*, 385). "The deepest stratum of our lives, the one which sustains and carries all the rest, is formed by beliefs. (Let us leave aside the question of whether below that deepest stratum there does exist something more, a metaphysical substratum which not even our beliefs can reach)" (*ibid.*, 388).

That this interpretation is not unfounded is confirmed, aside from the quotations given, whose meaning is quite clear, by the fact that in another work written in 1914, *Vieja y nueva política* [Old and new politics], the same intuition appears also, in a different context and form: "Fichte brilliantly said that the secret of Napoleon's policy and in general, the secret of any policy, consists simply in this: to declare what *it is*, where he understood *what it is* to be that underlying reality which constitutes in each epoch, at each moment, *the true and intimate opinion* of a part of society. We have all experienced how difficult it is to know which are *our true, intimate, decisive opinions* on the majority of things. We talk about them, we express opinions about them . . . but we notice that something in us resists recognizing those opinions uttered by our lips *as our opinions*. . . . And *it is not that we are lying;* this would imply that we say one thing while clearly thinking another. The only thing that we sincerely perceive is that *the dark and intimate depth of our personality* does not feel itself entirely bound to these opinions . . ." (*O.C.*, I, 269). And a little later he speaks of "those *unexpressed and intimate opinions* of a social group, of a generation, for example" (*ibid.*, 270). Those opinions which are not "what we think," about which he accumulates adjectives—true, intimate, unexpressed—are the *beliefs*, the familiar way in which the things that we foresee happen. This is something on which we count, as compared with which even what we actually see "seems incredible to us."

20. The fictional character is, then, the key to the unity of both worlds. This is a simple esthetic or "literary" consequence of the central *philosophical* discovery of this book: the world is *circumstance*, that is, *my* circumstance, and "I am myself plus my circumstance." In other words, the real world and the world of adventure *communicate* in the life of Don Quixote, whose circumstance they both are, and this makes *one world* of both—although precariously, because Don Quixote is mad. The only way of "connecting" both, so that the poetic character of the one is reflected on the other, is the creation of a character inserted into that dual "worldhood": dual by its origin, its nature, but with that

duality automatically annulled by the very life of the character because to live is to be in *one* world, and it is precisely human life
which establishes the connection between all the ingredients of the
real as *such a world*. Don Quixote belongs to reality, but his will
forms part of reality with him, and this is "the will for adventure."
He is "a frontier nature, as the nature of man generally is, according to Plato." (What makes possible the "coexistence" of Don
Quixote with "others" and, therefore, his circulation through the
"real" world is the intervention of Sancho, whose circumstance is
"in communication" with that of his master, although he remains
attached to the common reality; that is why the first time Don
Quixote sallies forth alone, he returns home downtrodden after
his first encounter, but when he is accompanied by his squire he
can reach Barcelona with a minimum of "normality." On this
function of Sancho, see my article "Don Quijote visto desde
Sancho Panza," *La Nación*, Buenos Aires, Oct, 30, 1955.)

21. This passage expands and expresses concretely the theory of
reality sketched earlier (cf. Note 13). There the "structure" was
considered as a peculiar reality, as a "thing in a secondary sense"
(elements plus order). In each thing we find *reflections* of and
connections with other things, and on this is based the depth, or
to express it differently, the "meaning" of each thing, which is
the highest form of its coexistence with other things; that is, it
is not enough to apprehend the *material* aspect of a thing, but its
meaning (the shadow which the rest of the universe casts on it)
is needed also. Now, Ortega distinguishes formally the *materiality*
of things (an expression he will replace in his maturity) understood as that which constitutes things before and above any interpretation, from their meaning, which is just *things when they
are interpreted*. There is, then, a bare reality previous to any
interpretation, and a reality which has been interpreted or has
meaning. Later on, Ortega says that circumstance presents itself
to us only as "nothing but the facilities and difficulties encountered
in living," onto which we have to project our plans, and thus interpret them and make "things" out of them. That is why he also
says that man "makes his world," he is a born builder of uni-
verses. We see now how Ortega elaborates this philosophical
theory *through Quixote*, by making this apparently literary analysis of Cervantes' work; hence the inseparability of the first
meditation from the rest of the book.

22. This example clarifies the previous statement: the windmills
rise and gesticulate above the horizon; this "reality" has a meaning,
that is, it has to be *interpreted*. One of these meanings or interpretations is the one which Don Quixote projects on them: they
are giants. The fact that Don Quixote is insane, that is to say, the

NOTES 185

fact that we invalidate his interpretation—from the viewpoint
of our own interpretation—does not affect in the least its interpretative character nor its internal mechanism; on the contrary, it poses the problem in more sharply defined terms. Consequently, Ortega goes on asking: "Granted that these giants are
not giants, but what about the others? I mean, what about giants
in general? Where did man get his giants? Because they never
existed nor do they exist *in reality*. . . . There would always be
something which was not a giant, but which tended to become
one if regarded from its idealistic side." Any "reality" to which
we may refer is a "meaning" and, therefore, an interpretation; so
is "materiality," just like any other form of reality. What is its
"meaning"? It is this: "the thing when it is not interpreted."

23. In the last few years people have talked a great deal in Spain—
and a certain amount outside of Spain—about Ortega's "cul-
turalism," a presumed tendency of his to "substantify" culture.
This very early passage is conclusive enough. It is an "illusion" to
try and see culture as a separate and self-sufficient world "to
which we can transfer our hearts," that is to say, one in which we
can settle our lives. Culture is nothing but an "illusion," a "mirage,"
and only when it is thus looked upon is it "put in its place." But let
it be understood that this is *what it must be*, this is its function,
and a *necessary* function, because that insufficient "illusion," which
has to support itself on an actual reality, is in its turn indispensable
to the latter. The fully-developed consequences of this point of
view may be seen in *Ideas y creencias* where fiction and science,
Hamlet and the triangle, are formally matched, and against which
the substratum of reality *in* which we live and which sustains us
is set up as a contrast.

24. Ortega distinguishes between two "realities": a primary one,
the "so-called" real; the other, an "objectivity," which is the
aggregate of all its interpretations, a "duplication" of the former.
It should be noticed that the character of reality is not just
ascribed to the inert and the uninterpreted: that these interpretations, far from being simple ideas, something subjective, are
defined as an *objectivity*, something which I find before me as
an object. He uses a significant word: the interpretations *coalesce*
into an objectivity; this coalescence is precisely what we might
call its "worldlification," the creation of a stratum of "consistent"
reality with which we have to cope. This is so much so that
Ortega goes on to indicate the everlasting "conflict" between the
"idea" or "meaning" and the "materiality" of each thing. In that
conflict, one of the antagonists triumphs over the other; the full
triumph of the idea supersedes the materiality; that is to say, it
imposes an interpretation *velis nolis*, although it may do violence

to the materiality. Then we live *under a hallucination* (this is Don Quixote's situation, and perhaps that of entire societies, to a lesser degree); the imposition of the materiality, on the other hand, its *reabsorption* of the idea, that is, the defeat of the interpretations by the inert thing, makes us live *disillusioned*. Here the word *illusion* retains the double character, positive and negative, which it has come to have in Spanish and in some other languages: it is both mirage, fiction, even deceit, and at the same time project, incitement, hope. This passage is another phase in the theory of the "reabsorption" of the self by the circumstance.

25. Realism is *also* a point of view, a perspective, an interpretation. Ortega accumulates images of perspective: distance, light, inclination, slope; and active verbs which indicate some action we perform: to bring, to put, to slant. Realism is as much our "invention" as idealism can be: a way of interpreting reality which stresses its material side—though it is not the only one, of course; and then, once interpreted thus, "the inert and harsh object rejects whatever 'meanings' we may give it," precisely because we have already given it *that one:* we have interpreted it as "mute, terrible materiality." This is why Ortega adds that the starting point of all poetry, including the realistic, is the *myth*. Realistic poetry consists in accompanying the myth in its descent, in its fall; it is "the collapse of the poetic." If "materiality" were the *sufficient* reality, nothing more would be necessary; but interpretation, "mythification" is needed—no matter what the nature of the myth. The "inertia and desolation" of reality, on becoming "an active and combative element," is the only thing which can bring it into the realm of art. Neither reality itself—things as such— nor its duplication interests us; all that interests us is its "drama" (this is what "active and combative" means), what happens to that reality when it confronts us in that struggle of interpretations, that is, as an ingredient of our lives. Hence the "indifference" of realism towards things: one is as good as another, because *they* are not interesting in themselves.

26. It is not necessary to insist on the philosophical importance of this text. The distinction between realities and reality is explained here as the difference between *things* and reality as a *generic function*, that is, what share they have of *reality*, what makes them "realities." Objects have "an imaginary halo around them"—their interpretations—and pure materiality shows under it; man aspires, loves, imagines; but all this yields before that "final resort" of their generic reality if *it is taken as sufficient*. What is represented in characters, that is, in the human drama, is *reality*. Now—and only now—can we fully understand a passage from the prologue: "When shall we open our minds to the con-

viction that the ultimate reality of the world is neither matter nor spirit, is no definite thing, but a perspective?" I have already commented on it in detail (cf. Note 6), but paying attention almost exclusively to the idea of *perspective*. It was not yet clear what Ortega meant by what he has called on occasion "the transcending of substantialism," an expression which is perhaps equivocal, but which at any rate may mean to go beyond *things* as ultimate reality to that on which they are based and from which they are derived. The decisive point is that the ultimate reality is "no definite thing"; in the present text, Ortega moves from "this or that thing" to reality as a generic function, from things to *their* reality. He says here that this generic reality is represented in characters, and he said before that the ultimate reality of the world is a perspective, two expressions which unmistakably point to the reality which is to constitute the central theme of Ortega's philosophy: *human life*. We shall see it appear still farther on under a third name, but in this first book, Ortega has not yet arrived at that expression, the simplest and most profound. (One should remember that no other philosophy, independent of his, has yet appeared, since what Ortega understands by *human life* is not the *Leben* of the *Lebensphilosophie*.)

27. Ortega is defining here the very roots of *realism*, the interpretation of reality from the concrete perspective of realism. And I cannot help remembering the central passage from Sartre's *La nausée*, the seed of existentialism, which appeared a quarter of a century later, and took up, almost literally, the same vision of things, although Sartre added a philosophical interpretation of his own with quite a different inspiration. I refer to the impressions of Antoine Roquentin in the *Jardin publique* when he discovers the meaning of *existence:*

". . . I can't endure any more, I'm stifling: existence is penetrating into me everywhere, through my eyes, my nose, my mouth . . .

". . . existence had suddenly revealed itself . . . it was the very stuff of things; . . . the diversity of things, their individuality was only an appearance, a varnish. This varnish had dissolved, leaving monstrous, flabby masses, in disorder—naked, with a frightening and obscene nakedness . . .

"This moment was extraordinary; I was there motionless and chilled, plunged into a horrible ecstasy. . . . Contingency is the essential thing. I mean that, by definition, existence is not necessity. To exist is simply *to be there;* existing beings appear, may be *met,* but one can never deduce *them* . . .

"It [existence] must invade you abruptly, it must sit upon you, it must weigh heavily on your heart like a big motionless beast— or else there is nothing at all anymore.

"Everything was complete, everything in action, there was no lax time . . .

"I was not surprised, I knew very well that this was the World, a completely naked World which appeared suddenly. . . . It did not make sense; the world was everywhere, present, in front, behind" ("Wednesday, 6 P.M.," *La nausee*, 1938.)

28. This short chapter introduces, in a still hesitant way and paying attention to a particular dimension—which, however, soon becomes essential—an embryonic theory of human life which will be completed later on with the analysis of another related dimension. The hero and tragedy, or in other terms, the heroic and tragic dimensions of human life, are the aspects in which Ortega begins to disclose the characteristics of human life in general. It suffices to connect these pages with the rest of the book and bear in mind their full development in later works for their real philosophical significance to be apparent.

29. Ortega analyses Don Quixote's sentence, according to which people can take good fortune away from him, but not his effort and courage. The adventure as success may be chimerical; his will is real and true. Therefore, the adventure—which is, above all, an adventure sought-after, *wanted*, whose essence is a "sallying forth in search of adventures"—carries within itself that duality: the real and the unreal coexist *as such* in it; it is "a dislocation of the material order," its two elements "belonging to opposite worlds" which coexist within it in a strange way. The adventure reveals, then, a certain manner of being in which the unreal as such acts on reality and is an ingredient of it. What is this manner of being?

30. We find here, even with its own special term, the idea of *project*, and it is defined literally by its *not being*, by its unreality. That "not being"—but trying to be—governs and makes up reality, rules and molds it. The man who wants adventure—and perhaps there are none who do not—is not satisfied with reality, he makes it and reforms it by virtue of that project which *is not*. Ortega opposes custom, tradition, biological instincts, to that project, that is, nature, society, and history, what there is of "real," of "thing"—*sensu lato*—in man. "These men," he concludes, "we call heroes." But it should be remembered that previously he has said: "All of us are heroes in varying degrees." (*Cf.* p. 41.) The heroic character belongs, then, "in varying degrees" ("what is human admits degrees," as he says in later writings and lectures) to all men, or in other words, the condition described belongs to all human life.

31. The hero is defined by his refusal to accept reality, that which

is, and by a will to alter reality; that is to say, a will for adventure. The latter is fundamentally a project, but a project for what? The many possible projects depend on one basic and essential one, which has oneself for its subject. It is about himself that the hero plans, and this project implies the others (*cf.* page 154). For that reason, heroism leads us to resist the impositions of heredity, of environment: "we seek to base the origin of our actions on ourselves and only on ourselves. The hero's will is not that of his ancestors nor of his society, but his own. This will to be oneself is heroism." He sets up against the pressure of society the *customs* of the present) or of the past (ancestors) the *selfness* of the hero who wants to be *himself* and to be the source of his own acts. This is a precise definition of *authenticity* and of its opposite, abandonment to inertia and collective pressures. Heroism in this context is exactly the same as authenticity. And this clarifies the meaning of the previous thesis: we are all to some degree authentic; life implies a certain degree of authenticity and a certain degree of inauthenticity. (*Cf.* the recent development of the idea of *Eigentlichkeit* [reality] or of *eigentliche und uneigentliche Existenz* [real and unreal existence] by Heidegger.)

32. Here we see reappear the idea of authenticity, this time as "profound originality," which is the practical or active originality, that is, the one in which the "hero" makes himself. And why does Ortega call the authentic man a "hero"? Justification for this term is not lacking, and he outlines it here: to be *himself*, man has to live in "perpetual resistance" to what is habitual and customary—to the pressures of society, custom, habit, to what the others do, that is, what everybody does (as in Heidegger's *man*, one). This form of life is "perpetual suffering," it is "tearing oneself away from that *part of oneself* given over to habit, a prisoner of matter" (the italics are mine); it is, above all, "to invent a new kind of gesture." Resistance against pressures, tearing oneself away from a part of one's own life, invention and project; this is what life as heroism means to Ortega in 1914. The German title which he gave to one of his last books is worth noting: *Der Mensch als utopisches Wesen,* man as a utopian being.

33. Ortega returns to the theme of authenticity (see Notes 31 and 32); the heroic has its root "in a real act of the will." This is contrasted with the epic, so that Don Quixote, without being an epic figure, is nevertheless a hero. "Achilles makes the epic, the hero wants it." There is a sentence in this passage which needs to be read with the greatest attention: "the tragic character is not tragic . . . in so far as he is a man of flesh and blood, but only in so far as he wills." Let us not forget that Ortega has just emphasized the *real* character of the act of will, and that he begins

by saying that what *that* man wants is *to be himself;* therefore he is tragic as far as *he wants to be himself.* This means that he is not dealing with man as a "thing," as a natural being "of flesh and blood," but as an *aspiration* or *project* about himself. For that reason he adds that "the will is the tragic theme," and explains that the will is "that paradoxical object which begins in reality and ends in the ideal, since *one only wants what is not*"; which shows that when he speaks of "will" he is not thinking of a psychic "faculty," which is completely real and not at all paradoxical, but of a *projective aspiration* which wants what is not—not *yet,* that is—which moves in the unreality of the imagined and programmatic.

34. This is a first step in the face of the dominant theories, influenced mainly by their consideration of Greek tragedy. Ortega has cautioned earlier against paying too much attention to Greek tragedy, founded as it is on half-explained religious hypotheses which we do not yet quite understand. If the tragic theme is the will as a project, and therefore as a free invention of man, this is not consistent with the idea that fate or destiny, fatality, *ananke, heimarmene* or *fatum* is the true mover of tragedy. If it were so, determinism could be a substitute for destiny; but what it actually does is to annul tragedy. The common spectator, says Ortega at this point, finds tragedy a little unlikely, because he thinks that "all the bad things happen to the hero through his persistence in such and such a purpose." And he concludes: "There is no fate, then, or rather what happens is fated to happen because the hero has caused it. The misfortunes of Calderón's *Constant Prince* were fated from the point when he decided to be constant, but he himself was not made constant by fate." That is to say, what happens to the hero happens *because he wants it,* that is, because *he wants to be himself,* because he has decided to be constant, because, as Sartre would say, perhaps inaccurately, "he has chosen himself" as constant. With one more step, Ortega reverses the terms: far from the intervention of fate being necessary, it is the will, liberty, that is necessary. "Far from the tragic originating in fate, then, it is essential for the hero to want his tragic destiny." There can be no doubt that Ortega refers to the "project," the "aspiration," the "vital program," the "fictional character," which make up the self according to his mature writings, nor is it necessary to do violence to the texts, because to those unmistakable ones already quoted, he adds this one: "the hero refuses to give up an *ideal part,* an *imaginary role* which he has *chosen.* The actor in the drama . . . plays a part which is, in its turn, the *playing of a part,* although the latter is played *in earnest*" (italics are mine). (If one reads carefully the chapters of Sartre's work closest to this theme, especially *L'être et le néant,* 1943, p. 77–127, and also

L'existentialisme est un humanisme, it can be seen how far he develops these ideas and how far he pushes them in a completely different direction.) There are still two points which require comment. One is the expression quoted above: "it is essential for the hero *to want* his tragic *destiny*." Ortega's whole doctrine of authenticity is summed up here, just at tl.e point where it differs basically from the developments which Sartre has given it. It is not a question of a pure and simple *choice* by man, still less of a *gratuitous* choice. Man feels himself "called" to be *somebody*, and this is the meaning of *vocation, destiny;* but this destiny is not *imposed* upon man, it is *proposed* to him. Man does not choose his destiny (it is destiny for that very reason), but he has to choose between *being or not being faithful to it;* in other words— as Ortega puts it—*to want it or not.* It is essential for the hero— the authentic man—to want it; *only he who wants his destiny*, who insists on being himself, *is authentic.* The other point is this: "an entirely free volition originates and produces the tragic process. This 'act of will,' *creating a new series of realities* which only exist through it—the tragic order—is naturally a *fiction* for anyone whose only desires are those of *natural* necessity, which is satisfied with what merely *exists*" (italics mine). Freedom engenders or "creates" an environment of realities different from the merely natural, with respect to which they are "fiction," and thus it introduces another kind of reality besides *what is*, a kind to which *what is not* essentially belongs, and that reality is precisely that of *human life.*

35. Here we have the formulation of a characteristic or requisite of human life: *the will to be what one is not yet.* This leads Ortega to add immediately: "The noble heroic fiction rises above the inertia of reality through the greatest exertions; it lives by aspiration. The future is its witness." This is what the philosophy of the last thirty years has commented upon in many different ways, including the inaccurate ones which forget part of what Ortega says here: that half the figure of man—the tragic character—is outside of reality, which means that it is *half inside.* Sartre, for example, writes: "I am not the one I shall be. Firstly, I am not because time separates me from it. Secondly, because what I am is not the foundation of what I shall be. Finally, because no present being can determine exactly what I am going to be. As, however, I am already what I shall be (otherwise I would not be interested in being one thing or another), *I am the one I shall be in the manner of not being it*" (*L'être et le néant*, p. 69). When he writes this, he is not saying anything different from what I have just underlined and commented upon in the preceding pages; nor when he speaks of "a first project about myself which is like my choice of myself in the world," or of the "unique and primary

project which constitutes my being" (*ibid.*, p. 77); nor when he says that "it is a question of establishing human reality as a being which is what it is not and which is not what it is" (*ibid.*, p. 97). But when, in the same context, he adds: "nothing can assure me against myself, cut off as I am from the world and from my essence by this nothing which I am" (p. 77); or else: "this being is constituted as human reality in so far as he is nothing but the original project of his own nothingness" (p. 121); or again: "If man, such as the Existentialist conceives him, is not definable, it is because he is nothing to begin with" (*L'existentialisme est un humanisme*, p. 22); or finally: "man is nothing but his project, he exists only in proportion to his realizing himself, he is nothing then but the sum total of his acts, nothing but his life." In these passages he draws radically away from what Ortega has thought from his first book and also, I think, from a successful solution (*cf.* my essay "El pensamiento y la inseguridad" [Thought and uncertainty] in *Ensayos de convivencia* [Essays on coexistence], 1955.

36. This passage, as I already remarked, establishes the connection between the two *Meditations* and in my opinion represents the culmination of the philosophical thought contained in this book, the most important thesis of which, already outlined in the prologue, is made fully understandable: "The reabsorption of circumstance is the concrete destiny of man" (*cf.* Note 7). When commenting on that passage, I had to anticipate the commentary on this one. It is only necessary to add some remarks arising from all that has gone before. "The hero," Ortega says, "made this (the tragic role) part of himself, he fused himself with it"; but now follows the "reabsorption by reality"—by the reality with which man has to cope, whether he wishes it or not, by the reality in which he finds himself and which he himself is—and that reabsorption "consists in solidifying, in materializing the aspiring intention of the hero upon his person." In other words, to the movement of the self which tries to "reabsorb the circumstance" and humanize it, is opposed the resistance of the latter which "reabsorbs the role or project," materializes it, solidifies it, turns it into a thing, makes it a perpetual aspiration and perpetual frustration ("man as a utopian being"). That is why human life is *drama* (not tragedy, Ortega says in his last writings, because tragedies are part of life itself); it is not exhausted by being a project, it is not *only* project, it is *circumstance* and *destiny* as well.